# EVERYDAY
## ENTREPRENEURS

Every owner of a physical copy of *Everyday Entrepreneurs* can download the eBook for free direct from us at Harriman House, in a DRM-free format that can be read on any eReader, tablet or smartphone – simply head to **ebooks.harriman-house.com/everydayentrepreneurs** to get your copy now.

# EVERYDAY ENTREPRENEURS

A SUGAR-FREE, DRAGON-SLAYING START-UP GUIDE
FOR THE SIMPLE SMALL BUSINESS

KEN HORN

HARRIMAN HOUSE LTD

3A Penns Road

Petersfield

Hampshire

GU32 2EW

GREAT BRITAIN

Tel: +44 (0)1730 233870

Email: enquiries@harriman-house.com

Website: www.harriman-house.com

First published in Great Britain in 2014

Copyright © Harriman House

Cover and internal images ©iStockphoto.com/pressureUA

The right of Ken Horn to be identified as the Author has been asserted in accordance with the
Copyright, Designs and Patents Act 1988.

ISBN: 9780857193452

British Library Cataloguing in Publication Data
A CIP catalogue record for this book can be obtained from the British Library.

*My sincere thanks go to Stewart McGloughlin of Sterling Tax and Nigel Starkey of TaxAssist for
their valuable contribution to the more taxing content.*

*I would like to dedicate this book to my wonderful wife Helen and my two boys James and Kerr.
Whatever I choose to do, their endless encouragement, belief and support provides timely
motivation and energy whenever doubt strengthens and stamina weakens.*

Harriman House

# CONTENTS

## ABOUT THE AUTHOR

Over the course of ten years, business advisor Ken Horn has helped thousands of people to be a success running their own businesses. With his help they have turned interests and skills into long-term, flourishing businesses – not setting out to conquer the world  like contestants on *The Apprentice* or *Dragons' Den*, but reaching freedom and financial security by delivering traditional services in existing markets. This is the world of the everyday entrepreneur – where you don't have to be starting an airline to make a living, or trying to invent the Next Big Thing before you get going. It's what 99% of start-ups set out to do – and what 99% of business books and advisors hardly ever discuss.

In his former life, Ken worked in the fast-moving consumer goods industry, supplying leading retailers, grocers and brands. He has closed businesses, sold businesses, developed businesses and in 2005 launched his own business following a failed acquisition of a leading sports distributor. Since then, Ken has lent his expertise to a range of leading business support agencies, colleges and universities.

In 2011 Ken launched a new nationwide business support platform called Kick Off in Business. Working with Premier and Football League clubs, the scheme has encouraged countless people across the country to set up their own businesses.

He has been featured on BBC Breakfast, ITV News and Channel 4.

# INTRODUCTION

A S A BUSINESS ADVISOR FOR THE PAST 10 YEARS I have worked with more than 5,000 people who wanted to start their own businesses. The vast majority were not intent on world domination but simply wanted to set up a conventional business supplying a traditional product or service. In fact, research suggests that this is easily the most popular kind of business formed in Britain every year.

So you might expect the business shelves in bookshops to reflect this mix. Instead, they're packed with the autobiographies of leading entrepreneurs like Sir Richard Branson and Lord Sugar. Don't get me wrong: these have their place. But in all the time I have been working with start-ups, I have never met a client looking to start an airline.

I'm convinced that most start-ups would get much more from observing, studying and sharing the experiences of other closely-related businesses. That's why the first thing this book attempts to do is to package up the common challenges and considerations of starting up and help readers tackle them. It is tidy, concise and uncomplicated.

The second thing this book does is to strip away much of the mystery surrounding starting your own business.

Most business support is now online, especially with the withdrawal of Business Link, the government-funded business advice service, in 2011. Now start-ups are faced with an ocean of remote information. It's confusing. How do you know what you need to know and what you don't? I run field-based events to help start-ups and almost everyone reports having problems with this.

Moreover, there are things that you need to know when you first start and things you need to know after 12 months, two years and so on. Online providers and other agencies attempt to provide you with all the information in one go. The result is a mess. Vital stuff gets missed, less vital stuff gets needlessly stressed over.

That's why this book provides you *only with what you really need to know to launch a small business, as well as revealing what can be left till later and in what order to best tackle things.*

It also reveals a whole host of secret shortcuts that are too easily missed – especially when it comes to sales and marketing.

If you want to start an airline (who hasn't thought about it at least once?), there are other books available. For everyone else, I think that *Everyday Entrepreneurs* is the quick-to-read, no-nonsense business book you've been waiting for.

**KEN HORN, 2014**

STUFF
BEFORE
Y O U
START

# ONE

Part one of this book explores some of the things you need to consider before you start your own business. I cover both soft topics such as skills, attributes and characteristics as well as some more tangible areas like pre-start expenses and other formalities.

It doesn't really matter how far away you are from launching your business. This advice is vital for people who have no intention to start trading for another year as well as people who have already been trading for 6–12 months. (It's amazing what can get overlooked.)

# 1. THE MOST EXCITING THING ABOUT BEING SELF-EMPLOYED

THE BIG BURNING QUESTION YOU NEED TO ASK yourself before you start is *what do you want from your business?*

People start businesses for a whole range of reasons, not always to do with money or wealth. In fact, of the thousands I have helped set up in business, very few placed wealth or money at the top of the list. In my experience, the most common reason people start a business is *satisfaction*.

On my office wall at home is a photograph of a cheque dated December 2005 for the grand total of £150. Why have I kept a copy? Well, I'm not particularly proud of the amount of work that I did for £150: it just symbolises a defining moment, the point when someone else was prepared to pay money for the services of something *I* had created. My business. My work.

This was hugely satisfying at the time and is still the principal motivation that gets me up on a cold, dark winter's morning. Not money.

The second most common reason people start businesses is… *control.* Not having to listen to other people. Being in charge of their own destiny. All that stuff.

The temptation for many start-ups is to look at the immediate aspects of control – i.e. getting up when I like, playing golf when I like, going to work in my pyjamas, etc. But it's only when you expand the notion of control that it gets really interesting. Being in business for yourself allows you to control the speed you travel, the direction you travel in, the size the business becomes or doesn't become.

No one else controls these things. You do. *That's* the most exciting thing about being self-employed.

# 2. TARGETS, VISION AND VALUES

G ETTING TO THE SATISFYING PLACE OF BEING OUR
own boss is not instantaneous. The good news is that it
is a lot easier than you might think. In fact, breaking it down
into easy steps is half the trick. The secret ultimately lies in
*targets, vision and values.*

## TARGETS

In the days of the old government-funded business advice
service, Business Link, because the government was picking
up the bill, we business advisors would offer to meet face-to-
face with clients every couple of weeks.

This was a very valuable service for the majority of clients.
Not only were they receiving qualified advice, but they were
getting it regularly. Often people implode worrying about the

weight of information they think they need to start a business. The Business Link process enabled advisors to break down much of this and package it into smaller, bite-sized chunks. Clients simply focused on a set of these items – and only a set – between biweekly meetings.

This worked well. Unfortunately, since the withdrawal of the Business Link service, this option is no longer available. **Nevertheless, the incremental process absolutely still works.**

So try to set yourself small incremental objectives – break everything down into little steps. It really helps. For example, if you have a target of £30,000 of sales in the first year, you can't just stop there:

- Before you generate any sales you'll need a customer.
- In order to generate a customer, you'll need to promote your services.
- If you're going to promote your services, you'll need some promotional material.
- To produce some promotional material, you'll need a menu of services.
- Therefore, one of the things you need to do is build your menu.

Start there.

The danger with most targets is that people set them too large or too far away and therefore lose sight of the steps needed to reach them.

## VISION

Having a vision for your business is also vital. But the mistake made by many start-ups is to create a vision and then place it on the bookshelf in an envelope never to be seen again.

Starting a business can be a lonely affair. Few people will be surrounded by fellow directors and employees when they first start. All decisions will be made in isolation and without the guidance of anyone else. **Having a vision for your business provides you with a guidance system, like a business satnav.** It reminds you where you're trying to go.

Through the course of the first 6–12 months, there will be lots of temptations, distractions and opportunities to deviate from your original plan. Targets can't get you away from these all the time. And sometimes, you may need to go beyond your targets. Your vision will keep you on the right track. It will help you to make the right decisions for your business. Even now, when I go into WHSmith's to buy a new marker pen, I think "Does buying this marker move me closer to my vision?"

## VALUES

And what about values? Even though you may be about to launch a traditional business, do you have a series of values that you intend to embed in the delivery of your service? You could have a particular environmental ethos, or a local focus, or something else altogether.

Some of the biggest organisations in the world have very clear values. Apple, for example, uses three words to describe its values: *Simplify, Perfect, Delight.*

The most powerful and useful thing about values is that, as your business grows, these values can be shared with new employees, customers and suppliers and will become an important part of the recruitment process for new staff and developing new services.

**In other words, targets get your business through the week, a vision gets you to where you want to go in the long term and values make sure you do all this in a way that is consistent and reliable.**

# 3. THE OVERNIGHT BUSINESS TRIAL

IT IS ALSO WORTH TAKING A MOMENT TO CONSIDER some of the challenges you will face when starting a new business. Whatever stage your business is at, you will always face fresh challenges. The key is to anticipate these challenges and devise ways to tackle or navigate them. Here are some of the challenges faced by other start-ups and how to deal with them.

## THE MOST COMMON CHALLENGES

**The most common challenges for start-ups are finance and confidence.** Believe it or not, these two things are linked.

First of all, let's look at confidence. Many people are unsure whether their plan will work. They spend endless amounts of time planning, researching and planning some more. When I worked for Business Link, the number of people who would ask me whether I thought their business would work was enormous…but who was I to say? There is a group of people in the community far better placed to judge whether your business idea will work. They're called **customers**.

The earlier you test your theory with them, the better. At some point, the theory must stop and practice begin. It is a fine judgement when to take this leap without looking under-prepared. It is equally dangerous to over-prepare, though, as one thing is for sure: your proposition will change the moment it hits the market.

I often ask the groups we work with: what is preventing you launching your business to the market tomorrow afternoon? Actually, in most cases, very little. Once you have thought about a business name and range of services or products, you can very quickly appear to be already trading with some simple, inexpensive tools such as business cards, leaflets and so on. Bill Gates sold Windows to IBM before he actually had Windows. This activity is called piloting or test trading.

How does confidence link with access to finance? Whether a grant, bank funding or a soft loan, each will require a robust business case – typically called a business plan. Without any piloting, test trading or sampling, the business plan is simply theory and forecast. Any proposition you present to a potential investor or finance provider will carry much more weight if it is supported by a field-based test-trading period.

So that's finance and confidence. By far and away **the most important and difficult challenge facing any start-up is finding the first customer.**

Try to measure customer relationships beyond simply monetary value. Customers are far more important than that. They provide you with valuable feedback about your offer. They are a source of market intelligence. They can provide information about the competition. Therefore always try not to race to the finish line too quickly in your attempts to get an order or a cheque.

When I first started many years ago, I provided my services for free at the beginning because I recognised the value of the relationship beyond an immediate financial return. That initial approach led to a six-month paid contract. So try to think in terms of moving the conversation along as opposed to chasing the pound.

Once you secure your first customer, take great comfort that you're doing something right. Don't be complacent, though: always look to refine and upgrade your offer regardless of current, and possibly short-term, success.

# 4. NOT JUST ABOUT WORLD DOMINATION

WHAT ABOUT THE SKILLS AND ATTRIBUTES NEEDED to be a success in business?

First of all, let's banish the myth that, unless you have a long list of specific characteristics and skills, you are unable to start a business. One of the things that inspired me to write this book was the way in which start-ups are portrayed on programmes like *Dragons' Den* and *The Apprentice*.

The media has a huge responsibility to better represent the real people starting conventional businesses and making an amazing success of it. Contrary to what such programmes would have you believe, business is not really all about high-octane world domination.

Having met over 5,000 start-up hopefuls, in my opinion anyone can start a business given the right guidance and support. You will already have skills and knowledge that, unbeknown to you, will help you once your business is up and running.

For this reason it can be a useful exercise to identify characteristics and skills that may be useful going forward, while reflecting on those in your toolkit already. **You basically need to determine what you already have, what you have but need to develop, and what you don't have but need to get.**

Unfortunately, if you have never been in business before you may not know what you need. So a useful starting point is to list all the disciplines and functions you think you will have to perform in a typical day once self-employed. How many different hats will you wear?

To help you get started, I would suggest that there are three central characteristics that I think will help you enormously during your early trading period, regardless of what else is needed. The good news is that these are not rocket science and many people already possess them to some extent.

Briefly, the three core characteristics of successful entrepreneurs are:

1. Organisation.

2. Creativity.

3. Bouncebackability.

Given the sheer number of plates you will need to spin when you eventually launch your business, organisation will play a big part. So **if you're currently disorganised...get organised.**

Creativity is important because you *will* encounter obstacles and challenges during this important period. **The trick is to anticipate hurdles and devise clever ways to get over them.**

For example, your initial contact with a customer may result in a rejection. So start to value customers beyond simply people who pay you for your services. Customers are much more valuable than that, even the ones that reject you – because there is no law to say they will not consider you again in future, and even that rejection provides you with vital, authentic feedback. *Each customer exchange is an opportunity for you to refine your offer.*

Unfortunately, unless you are Steve Jobs, not everyone will like or buy what you have to sell (and even Steve didn't always get it right). J. K. Rowling had a number of failed attempts before finding a publisher. Despite this, Rowling learned from these earlier encounters – and the rest is history.

Other than determination and belief, I think the other thing Rowling had was one of the most important characteristics for any new business – resilience, or as I prefer to call it **bouncebackability.**

# 5. WHAT ARE YOU REALLY SELLING?

OVER THE YEARS WORKING WITH START-UPS I HAVE met a large number of people who would like to be self-employed but are not quite sure whether their idea is strong enough or simply don't have any idea what type of business to choose.

In fact, the people I meet fall into three categories:

1. They have a very fixed idea.

2. They have no idea.

3. They have oodles of ideas.

For all three categories, another useful exercise to consider doing as part of the pre-start process is to **observe what trends, fashions and movements are happening in the market.**

This will not only help those unsure what to do by beginning to steer them towards the more interesting prospects or helping fire ideas in their heads, but will also help those people who are already fixed on an idea by forcing them to sharpen and develop it.

A good early marketing trick can also be to try and associate your business with some of these trends (where it makes sense). It can be a little tough when you first start out to secure an initial customer and this can be a handy shortcut. Even just cosmetically aligning yourself with one or two trends for a short period of time can be a way of 'barging' into people's view.

**But perhaps most important is to work out what you're really selling.** Often you're not really – or not *primarily* – selling what you might think you are. For instance, take coffee shops. They sell coffee, right? So why aren't they stripped-down, bare-concrete rooms with plastic chairs and plywood tables and a single metal counter on the far wall with a functional but ugly-looking coffee machine making vaguely threatening gurgling sounds?

They are warm, vibrant, welcoming places filled with leather sofas and thick carpets and coffee-makers like gleaming spaceships because coffee shops aren't really selling coffee – they're really atmosphere and lifestyle shops with a good sideline in caffeine. Getting the caffeine (or ultimate product) right is hugely important, but you need to nail the preliminary offer too.

A great example of someone getting to grips with this issue is a client of mine called John, a 54-year-old gardening enthusiast from Leicester. John wanted to offer gardening services three days a week and had decided to exclusively target a very specific group (actually against my advice): the elderly.

Cleverly, John had nurtured a relationship with a number of local garden centres and thought it would be a great idea to erect a banner or flip-up stand in the front entrance of each of the centres. The big question was: what would he put on his banner?

John understood very early on that he was not just selling gardening services. *He was also selling honesty, integrity, security and friendliness.* John was asking people to pay him to go onto their land when they were there and when they were not. Being trustworthy was critical – particularly if he wanted to sell his services to potentially vulnerable elderly people.

So, apart from his contact details and business name, John needed a banner image that communicated his message. What did he choose? Gardens? Flowers? Secateurs?

Remember his key goal.

After he had dismissed the idea of using a picture of his 17-year-old grandson – complete with Beats headphones, baseball cap and gold Renault Clio in the background – he settled on a picture of himself.

This turned out to be a masterstroke. There are few things as personal and which show that you have nothing to hide as a picture of yourself.

His strapline was: "*Hello I'm John, I look after your garden*". He also got a CRB badge placed on the top right-hand corner of his imagery.

And John got tons of work off the back of this. All because he researched his market and tailored his proposition to specifically reach out to them and *all* that they were looking for.

Of course, this process of watching the market and adjusting your business offer according to movements and trends and your target customers is not exclusive to start-ups. Established businesses always need to be ahead of the curve and have to be ready should the market change, move or dissolve. **It's the business adage: change or die.** Build it into your business from the start and you'll be ahead of many.

# 6. A GOVERNMENT
# HEALTH WARNING

SOMETHING YOU WON'T HEAR ON AN HMRC WORKSHOP or webinar is: **being in business is about eroding profit when and where you can.** The British business tax system is designed to tax any profit you make: therefore if you don't make any profit, you will pay little tax. Just look at Google or Starbucks!

There are only two ways I know to erode profit as a small business:

- reduce your prices
- build in costs.

Whilst capturing costs will be important once trading begins, one group of costs you can build into your first year of trading is *pre-trading expenses* – costs incurred in setting up or researching your business even before you start. Tax rules allow you to claim these costs as if they were incurred on your first day of trading.

Another closely guarded secret by HMRC is how far back you can go to recover these set-up expenses. **You are able to go back seven years to recover any costs associated with setting up your business.** This may end up a sizeable sum – it's important to capture all of these costs.

*The vital question, however, is: what costs can I include?*

If you ask HMRC this question, they'll tell you to go and read the website which, on average, may take most people around four days. It's impossible to get anyone from HMRC to provide a form of words that best describes what you can and cannot count as a legitimate business expense. Once you have read this book you will have much more important things to do than drown in the sea of information at **hmrc.gov.uk**.

Having worked closely with HMRC in a former life, the following explanation closely reflects the rules surrounding pre-start expenses.

If you go into WHSmith's and buy a marker pen, the question you need to ask yourself is: "Does my business need this pen and can I evidence it?" Evidence is a double-edged sword. In the VERY unlikely event that an HMRC inspector has some free time left over after chasing MPs and you are investigated, it means you will need to prove that (a) the business had a need for the item and (b) that you have or had the item.

Please note the absence of the words "bought", "purchased" or "receipt".

This of course goes beyond physical items and may include services, travel and/or other types of expenses such as research (which we'll discuss later). HMRC would always prefer you to have the inside leg measurement and shoe size of the person that sold you the item but in most cases will accept that you have the item or can 'evidence' (a ghastly but unavoidable verb) that the expense was incurred or service provided.

In other words, even though you may have lost the receipt, can you still evidence you made that trip to London and that it was a necessary trip to help launch your business? If so, charge it to your business. Travel expenses are a large business cost and need to be deducted before any profit is declared. One effective way of evidencing pre-trading expenses is to keep a diary or a notebook and record the costs, especially cash transactions.

What about personal items that you own but the business now needs? The most common examples of these are laptops, PCs and tablets. Let's say you already own a smartphone and iPad when you decide to set up a business. You need to use both in your business, so do you:

(a) go and buy new items, or

(b) use the ones you already have?

You might not have the funds to buy new, but the business now draws value from an item you already own, so should you claim anything for giving the items to your business?

If you can evidence that the business needs an item that you already own, you may be able to get tax relief. No cash actually changes hands, of course, but you can claim what are called

'Capital Allowances' based on the approximate market value of the item on the first day you start trading. eBay might be a good place to check out the range of market values on an iPad or smartphone of similar age, for example, and you can always print screenshots as evidence to support the (highest) market value available.

The mistake many start-ups make is that they fail to recognise that they can claim tax relief on items they already own and start to use in their business.

This principle also applies to items on monthly contracts. Let's say shortly after starting up you realise that you need a new iPhone and you opt for an unlimited access tariff because, like most businesses, your business relies heavily on customer correspondence. This tariff includes unlimited broadband, unlimited texts and calls but the primary reason you have the all-singing, all-dancing tariff is because your business needs it. What happens if you accidentally use one of your unlimited calls to order a pizza or book cinema tickets?

Because itemised bills are now mostly consigned to history, HMRC is no longer empowered to request a full breakdown of business versus personal calls but generally any 'incidental' private use may be ignored. If you follow this logic, the same applies to other monthly subscription services such as home internet access or even satellite TV. **Providing you can evidence that the reason you MUST have super-duper fast broadband from BT is primarily for business purposes, the fact that your teenagers might incidentally access Xbox games at twice the speed of light is probably irrelevant – as long as they don't use it more than you do for business.**

## THE THREE-MONTH WINDOW

OK! Honeymoon over and you're now ready to launch your business. Once again, HMRC doesn't promote the fact that you have three months of trading before you need to notify any of the authorities. As we'll explore later, this provides valuable time to plan and research some important topics.

*What you need to ask yourself here is: when have I started?*

There are countless ways to define launching a business – from raising your first invoice to accepting payment for your goods or services. Unfortunately, there's only one that matters. The formal definition of trading according to HMRC is best illustrated by a shop. If a shop opens its doors tomorrow morning but nobody walks through those doors for six months, is the business trading or not?

Of course, it's trading from the moment its doors are open.

**HMRC regard trading as being from when you first offer your service or products for sale.** Clearly not all businesses are shops; the equivalent could be offering a business card, erecting a poster, paying for a local advert or even creating and publishing a website.

Regardless of business type, you have three months from this point before you need to choose which type of business you would like to create and tell the relevant authority. We'll go into exactly how to do that in *9. What type of business do you want (or need)?* But please note that if you miss the three-month deadline HMRC will charge you a penalty, so don't leave this chore to the last minute.

THE
NITTY-
GRITTY

TWO

Who do I tell?

When do I tell them?

Do I need this?

Do I need that?

What should I call myself?

What can I call myself?

This part of the book answers all of these questions. It also avoids some topics which, in my experience working with typical start-up businesses, are either less important or are not a serious consideration right now – e.g. the mechanics of employing lots of people or health and safety certification. These may become a consideration when the business reaches a certain size or age. For now, there are other priorities.

# 7. DO YOU NEED A BUSINESS PLAN?

EVERYONE NEEDS A BUSINESS PLAN, DON'T THEY? It seems to be the first rule of business advisory services or start-up gurus to say that they do. But actually, it's probably not true. Business plans are great, but I'm not someone who says that *everyone* needs one.

The fact is, some businesses are straight up-and-down – like tradespeople or IT repair. **And it's much better for straightforward businesses to concentrate on specific parts of a plan such as sales or promotion** rather than composing something like *War and Peace* only with more malfunctioning routers in it. It will only end up on a shelf gathering dust.

That said, there *are* some good reasons to put a plan together and not every business can ignore them.

## MONEY, MONEY, MONEY

*The principal reason for putting a business plan together is finance.* Whether we like it or not, the only language people in bank-land understand is a plan.

If you are going to beg, steal or borrow *any* amount of money – whether it's £50K from RBS or £50 from Job Centre Plus – you're going to need to put a plan together. It typically follows that the more you want to borrow, the bigger and deeper the plan has to be.

A common mistake people make is that they think the process of accessing grants or benefits is any different. But remember: a bank has a vested interest in giving you money (as long as it thinks you can repay it) because it will make interest on what it loans you. A grant or benefit provider *gives the money away.* The process is therefore often more difficult, requiring an even more robust argument to get the cash.

## THE WELCOME SKELETON

Another common reason people find planning useful is to provide some structure to the process of creating their business.

When you first start out towards having your own business, there is often a huge amount of noise and confusion. A plan can provide a breakthrough by helping you make sense of some of this noise. It allows you to organise your thoughts and research. It can also throw up areas that you haven't looked at closely enough yet, or issues you wouldn't otherwise think of.

A good business plan is really a bit like a skeleton for your business.

## THE PARTNER DILEMMA

Unfortunately I have met more people than I can mention who have set up in business with someone else only to see the business fall apart at an early stage. One of the reasons for this is that the individuals had different intentions for the business. If you are planning to go into business with someone else, it is a good idea to create a common reference point – and a business plan is a good common reference point.

## PERFORMANCE MONITORING

Of course, a plan is not just about the period before you start. Large established businesses still produce annual business plans. Naturally, a plan before you start is simply a theoretical device which, providing you have calculated the numbers correctly, displays a theoretical profit in the first or second year (*if it doesn't, amend until it does*).

You may have heard the expression "businesses go bust because they run out of cash". The more truthful expression is "businesses go bust because the management allow them to run out of cash". This is true. **Therefore a business plan becomes an essential management tool to monitor business performance once you start trading.**

It helps you ensure reality comes to reflect the theory and you actually make a profit. In the event of a mismatch, the responsible business manager can then take evasive action.

# 8. HOW TO CREATE A BUSINESS PLAN

THERE ARE PLENTY OF BUSINESS PLAN TEMPLATES available on the internet and elsewhere. The best advice I can offer is: *if you are planning to borrow money from an organisation or a bank, use their plan.* It talks their language, works with their systems, you can often access and adjust it live – and, of course, it has their branding all over it. This makes them feel all warm inside.

But if you're creating your business plan in the wild – or just want to start without being particularly committed to a particular lender – here's how you do it.

A typical business plan includes the following headings:

- business details
- business goals

- distribution
- legal
- key personnel
- marketing
- sales
- premises
- suppliers
- financials
- executive summary.

The topics in a business plan usually follow a particular order. Before we pick up on a few of these topics, there is something important that's missing. Imagine you are a bank manager and you have a pile of business plans in your in-tray – each indistinguishable from each other, boring black-and-white collections of paper.

*What's missing?*

A title or cover page. This is a small but easily avoidable mistake. Try to use this to bring the whole plan to life, especially if you have an easily illustrated or dramatic product you can stick on the front.

## GETTING IT RIGHT

OK, the sequence of a typical business plan – it doesn't change much but it's important to get it right. Most people will have watched *Dragons' Den* at some point. I'm not a great fan of the programme because it can misrepresent the true start-up funding process and really only improves the profile of the investors. Nevertheless, we can learn something from the typical order of a *Den* business pitch.

## EXECUTIVE SUMMARY

The first thing you need to provide in a business plan is a **summary of your business.** Again, avoid imitating 19th century Russian novels: a single A4 page detailing what you're going to do, who you're doing it for and – if finance is required – how much (exactly) you're going to need. This is called an *executive summary.*

## KEY PERSONNEL

If you reflect on the *Dragons' Den* process, what's the first question after the entrepreneur has introduced their idea? Often a dragon (usually Theo in the old days) will say: "Tell me about yourself and the people involved in your business."

At this point, *it's good to bear in mind that banks like teams, not individuals.* Even if having a few more names down is something of a cosmetic exercise (your brother the social media expert, your friend the logo designer, your aunt the accountant, etc.), it can be useful to make it look like you are not on your own. These people do not need to be directors or shareholders, they can simply be associates, friends or family members who have a skill or expertise useful to your business.

Indeed, beyond creating the right impression to an investor, it is not a bad idea generally to surround yourself with people who have complementary skills or can fill gaps in your expertise. I was once asked by the BBC to comment on a report produced by a large insurer claiming that the value of free advice offered to friends and family in the course of a year was £8.5 million. Yikes.

### BUSINESS DETAILS

Once the executive summary and key personnel are out of the way, it's onto business details. In other words, **where the business operates from and what legal structure the business will take** (don't forget, we'll be covering how to choose that just a little later).

A tip here is to list all the ways in which you will be visible to customers. Avoid the temptation to only put your mobile phone number as a contact point. A bank or investor wants to see as many ways as possible for you to receive enquiries – Twitter, Facebook, a website, email, mobile, landline, LinkedIn, etc.

### FINANCIALS

I'm going to break the sequence slightly at this point but with good reason. Have you ever presented a plan for finance or funding (perhaps just in the ordinary course of employment or in a former life)? If so, you will have noticed a very annoying thing that banks and other finance providers do. Instead of reading through all the pretty pictures and interesting narrative you have spent weeks compiling, they move straight to a section that is typically at the back and commonly referred to as The Financials.

Naturally, finance providers put a great deal of emphasis on the numbers and unfortunately this is the area that most people find challenging. It's a good idea to get it right early on, even if the final pages will sit somewhere at the back of the plan.

The financials are typically made up of three sections:

- a sales forecast

- a cash flow forecast

- a profit and loss (P&L) statement.

The sales and cash flow forecasts feed into the P&L and therefore it is the P&L that any bank or investor will target first. They'll then look for a particular line on the P&L: your projected profit (or loss), from which they'll make a very quick assessment based on information you provided earlier in the plan.

You may recall the Executive Summary included an amount you said you need to start your business. What the funder is quickly measuring is your ability to service the amount you have borrowed, or as they call it 'how well you can service the debt'. *A common mistake is for start-ups to declare they are likely to repay the debt very quickly.* They are then surprised when the bank says **NO!**

Remember, banks and many other finance providers are in business to make money from your borrowing. They are not likely to make much from you if you plan to repay your debt within three months. They normally prefer a plan that illustrates a 2–3 year repayment.

Once the reader is happy you can service the debt, they're now looking for evidence to support the P&L. The second most important entries on the P&L are the profit (or loss) and the sales you hope to generate. In most businesses, profit is driven by sales value and volume, so **attention quickly moves from the bottom line (profit) to the top line (sales)**.

However, the top line is simply a number, so more evidence will be needed to support that line...and that's where the sales forecast comes in. We'll also look at sales forecasting in more depth later, but for all intents and purposes this is a spreadsheet full of meaningless numbers.

### MARKETING AND SALES

The sales or marketing forecast or plan is probably the most important section of all. All business considerations – costs, employees, profit – are determined by sales. The reader is looking to the sales plan to find evidence for the claims made on the financial spreadsheet.

### BACK TO FRONT

If you haven't already spotted it, your business plan soon starts being read back to front. This is typical of any finance provider. So the trick is to construct robust financials and then use a lovely narrative to support these financials. (Some advisors even recommend that clients write their plans back to front.)

# 9. WHAT TYPE OF BUSINESS DO YOU WANT (OR NEED)?

AS I MENTIONED EARLIER, WE'RE NOW GOING TO pick out a couple of topics we've only touched on in passing as they are issues that challenge many new start-ups. The first area we're going to look at is what type of business you want (or need) to establish from a legal perspective.

There are a number of choices, subject to a range of considerations:

- sole trader

- partnership

- limited liability partnership

- limited company

- social enterprise.

Before you select which business type best suits your business, we first need to compare the key characteristics of each option, starting with the most popular choice for 80% of new start-ups: sole trader.

## GOING IT ALONE

So let's imagine we have reached the end of the three-month honeymoon period mentioned earlier and we now need to alert the authorities. In the case of sole traders, it's easy, quick and painless. You can either go online (**www.hmrc.gov.uk**) or call HMRC's self-employed helpline, and within four or five minutes you're on the radar.

The key point to observe as a sole trader is that while you have a choice over the year-end date for your accounts, your tax is generally calculated according to tax years, so it is always a good idea if your business accounting period is the same as the tax year, which runs April to April in any given year.

The spooky thing about being a sole trader is that it will be some time after that when you need to submit any records. Even though your year-end date might coincide with the tax year-end, 5 April, you are then given until 31 January the following year before you must file your self-assessment return online. (*Note:* if you prefer to submit a paper tax return it must reach HMRC by 31 October.) And of course if you miss these deadlines then HMRC will impose penalty charges, which can be expensive.

Let's imagine you start a business in May this year. You will prepare accounts for the tax year ending in April, but you'll have all the way to 31 January the following year before you have to file your tax return and pay any tax due. This is why HMRC sees a large increase in business registration in April and May each year – people wait to take advantage of this. In a later section we will explore the tax implications of sole trading and how it compares with other business structures.

Sole trading is far and away the most popular choice for people just starting up because of how simple and undemanding it can be. The biggest difference between being a sole trader and other business types comes with the issue of liability. When you register as a sole trader you are registering under your own name and any liabilities of the business rest with you. **In other words, any action or claim or debt held against the business becomes your problem.** Although this sounds very scary, remember that there are lots of insurance policies out there to protect you from such eventualities – and, if sole trading was such a nightmare, why do eight out of ten people choose it in the first place?

## THE PARTNERSHIP PARADOX

HMRC has seen a dramatic reduction in the number of partnerships registered in recent years. There are some good reasons for this. I wish I had a pound for everyone I've met who has just been through a failed partnership; they are notoriously problematic.

Partnerships are also heavier on administration than sole trading, and although they require a partnership agreement, this can be an oral agreement (but usually there's a bit of paper that clearly spells out the responsibilities of each partner). The danger with this is that, as a small business, people need to be versatile and able to adapt to different functions. Why would you want an agreement from the start that restricts this need?

If you really want to work with someone you can avoid a partnership arrangement simply by creating a shared identity, or a joint venture – where you have a brand or name above the door but operate independently underneath that brand and keep separate business records as sole traders.

## THE BRILLIANT OFF-THE-SHELF BUBBLE

But perhaps the main reason for the shortage of partnerships is that limited companies have raised their game. Gone are the days of paying an accountant £250 to set up a company and a minimum of £2,500 to set up the accounts. Limited companies have become a lot more user-friendly over recent years and offer a much more adult legal framework as a business structure.

As the second most popular choice for new businesses, it's only fair we look at the pros and cons of these too. Before that, though, let's look at the sequence of events in setting up your business. Remember the three-month honeymoon in telling HMRC you have started trading as a self-employed individual? The same applies to your company but in order to create the company identity, stationery, promotional material, etc., you may need to register the company early or as soon as you offer your service or product.

The internet is full of deals and company formation agencies, but my advice is to go to the government's business registrar direct: **www.companieshouse.co.uk**. Over the past few years, Companies House has improved its operational systems massively and forming a company is a relatively painless process that will only cost you around £15. HMRC is notified when a new company is formed, so they will automatically send you the necessary paperwork to register for Corporation Tax and report the trading start date.

Let's say you register a company on 4 July. Your year-end date becomes 31 July the following year. After you reach the year-end date, the company has ten months in which it must submit the company accounts to Companies House. It has 12 months to submit its Corporation Tax Return to HMRC. But the weirdest thing is it must pay any tax due within nine months of the year-end.

Many people are drawn to limited companies because of the potential tax advantages, but as far as commerciality is concerned the more important reason for trading as a limited company is protection.

Remember, a company is a legal framework in its own right, so any action, debt or claim against the business cannot be made against you personally. Any personal assets or effects are protected from contamination (unless it can be shown that you acted irresponsibly or negligently in managing the company's finances, which is another story altogether). You've no doubt seen cases in the news or had experience personally of people who are able to shut down a business on a Friday and start up the same business in the same market on the Monday under a different name. That is because they are able to dump all the liability, debt and dead wood into the previous operation and start up in a cleaner, meaner form a day later. Providing you can demonstrate that you did everything within your power to avoid that eventuality, then in most cases you really can just walk away.

This built-in protection that comes with a limited company also influences other business needs and opportunities. Let's say you're setting up a skydiving business. Will your insurance be cheaper or more expensive as a sole trader or as a limited company? If you think about it, in the event that something goes wrong, the liability and claim is unrestricted and would bleed into a sole trader's personal assets, making it difficult to contain the financial damage. With a limited company, the financial damage would be contained within the value and resources owned by the company – therefore there is a limit to the damage. For this reason, insurers prefer limited companies as any liability they face has boundaries. That's why their full names are actually 'limited liability companies'.

Another good argument for setting up a limited company is contractual. In the event that your business seeks to approach or trade with public sector authorities or large corporates you will find that many of them have supply chain criteria that includes the need for you to be a limited company. Why? If you have limited liability, so does your customer. And a supply chain full of limited companies usually makes for cheaper insurance.

SOCIALITES

The final choice of business type is social enterprise, legally known as a CIC or community interest company, and again this can be set up through Companies House.

What's the difference between a CIC and a limited company? A common mistake is to think it makes you a not-for-profit organisation, i.e. you don't need to worry about making money. This is again misleading. If you're not for profit, you're probably bust.

What it really means is that you make profits (good) but then you reinvest those profits for the good of the business and the service it provides. You also need to be able to demonstrate you provide a social benefit or value.

What separates social enterprises from other types of organisation such as charities is that charities shake tins, but social enterprises must trade – buy and sell or create a service or product to sell.

An increasing number of people who don't aspire to have a yacht or Caribbean holiday home are choosing to set up social enterprises. The principal attraction is that proposing to benefit society can make accessing funding, grants and other forms of finance a bit easier.

CICs are a little bit more involved than the standard business types. For this reason there are a number of regional agencies in place to help people develop them.

These agencies will help you in a number of ways. Firstly, they will test whether you have a social enterprise or not. Secondly, they will help you navigate the nitty-gritty involved in setting up. Finally, and most importantly, they will provide guidance on how and where to go to maximise the chances of securing finance.

# 10. WHAT MAKES FOR A SUCCESSFUL BUSINESS NAME?

THERE ARE TWO MAIN THINGS TO THINK ABOUT WHEN choosing a business name – legalities and image. This chapter will deal with both. However, despite the following advice, one thing I would like to stress is that, as someone courageous enough to set up on your own, you pretty much deserve to call yourself or your business whatever you like providing it's within the laws of England and Wales.

There are many challenges when developing a business, but one of the sexy bits is deciding on a name. My advice here is just advice. Naming your business can be a personal thing, but there are some common threads running through successful business names.

## PASSING OFF

Before we look at what makes for an effective name, let's quickly deal with the legal side of things.

Say I'm travelling down a well-known highway and I come across a guy selling burgers. Above his caravan, he has a piece of driftwood with the word *McDonalds* scrawled across it. We later establish he is a sole trader. Is he doing anything wrong, breaching any rules?

Strangely, no.

As a sole trader there is no formal register for business names. Moreover, his surname is McDonald. However, the minute he adds to the driftwood a couple of golden arches, he's in all sorts of trouble: that is a breach of copyright or trademark law.

So we must draw a clear distinction between business names and trademarks or copyright. But you still can't just call yourself what you want. The issue at question here is 'passing off', which basically means that you must never be able to be accused of using someone else's identity or mark in order to gain market share. If you do, you can be subjected to unimaginable pain.

So ask yourself: *if I call myself this, can I be accused of passing off?* If the answer is yes, don't.

When it comes to registering a company, *not* a sole trader, there is a hurdle at the start of the process that prevents you from naming your business in a way that conflicts with another or attempting to create an impression that you are something that you're not – e.g. a college or other institution. Instead of simply authorising such names, Companies House will either turn them down or ask you to prove you qualify for them.

While we're on the subject of law, there is a huge amount of confusion surrounding copyright and patenting. Copyright normally covers a piece of work like this book and patenting typically covers an invention, an item or process.

**Once again, a note of caution:** I have met too many people who have spent £2,500 with a local lawyer only to be told that their item cannot be patented. An alarming number of items are refused by the Intellectual Property Office (**www.ipo. gov.uk**) each year. So do make sure you speak to them before incurring any legal fees.

Moreover, the process of patenting is often misrepresented by programmes like *Dragons' Den* where investors will dismiss an investment because a patent has not been secured. They know that the process of application can be protracted and the danger is that the market opportunity moves faster than the process. The trick is not to miss the opportunity by standing around on ceremony – patenting isn't the be all and end all.

The case of Dutch satnav-makers TomTom is a good example. TomTom knew from the start that it could not protect the intellectual property behind satellite navigation. Instead its strategy was to hit the ground hard, fast and aggressively to establish itself as the market leader before anyone else was able to catch up. It's difficult to argue that this strategy has been unsuccessful.

## THE SEXY STUFF

Enough of the legal stuff about business names, what about the sexy stuff – what makes a good business name?

A huge amount has been written on this subject, and of course a recent trend is to select a name with no immediate reference to the nature of the business at all. But here are some more conventional guidelines for what makes a good business name:

1. *Describe it.* The 'Ronseal' approach – it does what it says on the tin. With the increased importance of online marketing and search engine optimisation, it can be valuable to have at least a partial description of what your business does in its name. Equally, think how often your business name appears without you actively trying to promote it: in a local authority register, in your address, in the free entry in *Yellow Pages*, etc. In such circumstances, a descriptive name does the marketing for you.

2. *Personalise it.* If you are planning to start a business that calls upon your personal experience, this can be important. You will more than likely have a reputation in your chosen sector or industry. We are often uncomfortable referring to ourselves as brands but in this case you really *are* the brand, I'm afraid, so you need to use it. Don't make the mistake I once made and call yourself something completely unrelated. The other reason why this is an important device is for the same reason discussed earlier with John, the gardener. John is providing a service and needs to quickly establish a relationship with his target audience. Using your own name gets you to this point with speed.

3.  *Localise it.* This may not be appropriate for everyone, particularly those with a national or international offer. Nevertheless, as consumers we are buying more locally. Even supermarkets are a good example of this, with some of them now allocating a whole aisle to locally-sourced products. Of course, they will tell you that they are driving this initiative but the truth is – *we* are. Localising can be done outside of the business name with things like telephone numbers. I have a plumbing and heating client who has a local number registered in each of the main areas of the West and East Midlands. He has one central phone operative taking diverted calls from each of these areas. Nevertheless, he appears to be local to each of those areas, which fits with the type of business he offers – people typically use a plumber within a 30-mile radius.

# 11. USING PROTECTION

EARLIER WE TOUCHED ON HOW ONE OF THE BEST-kept secrets in business is that you are allowed to trade for three months before you need to notify the authorities – HMRC, Companies House, etc. However, because even your test trade period will involve the delivery of your products or services, there is something you should get set up from the start: insurance.

As you'd expect, there can be lots of confusion about what types of insurance you need. Fortunately, common sense can usually help you out. For example, the law says I need employer's liability insurance – but this only applies if I have employees.

Nevertheless, there is one type of insurance every business should have from the start: public liability insurance. Although it's not technically mandatory, I would advise all businesses to get public liability insurance. It covers you for all those ridiculous eventualities that will never happen to you but to someone else. But it's a good idea.

The nature of your business will determine whether you need any other forms of insurance. The second most popular is product liability insurance. This only really applies if you are making (or buying) and selling products. If you are not making products but simply sourcing from another supplier, check that they carry their own product liability insurance.

The next most commonly purchased form of insurance is professional indemnity insurance or PII. This type of insurance is specifically for people like me who provide advice or instruct people. If a client acts on the advice we have provided and it is proven to be wrong or incorrect, that client may incur damage. We therefore need to indemnify them in the unlikely event that this happens.

Before you fall off your chair – and unless you are starting, say, a children's skydiving business – all these insurance policies usually don't break the bank. My combined policy of PII and public liability insurance costs me around £240 a year for £10m cover.

WHERE TO GET INSURANCE FROM

The insurance market is very competitive and is dominated by a number of well-known providers, from Tesco to Direct Line. The best advice I can give you is to talk first to trade associations or membership alliances. Not only are these people buying insurance on behalf of lots of people like you, making it cheaper, but it is likely to be tailored better to your type of business. Check out your local chamber of commerce for cheap insurance as well.

# 12. HOME AND HEADQUARTERS

THERE WERE SOME NOTABLE ABSENTEES FROM OUR discussion of insurance: home insurance and car insurance. These need to be dealt with a little separately as they involve broader considerations around using your house or personal car for business purposes, which is what this chapter is all about. Let's look at what you need to do.

## WHO TO TELL

First of all, let's get insurance out of the way. You should always inform both your house and car insurer that you intend to use your home or car for business purposes. Talk to your home insurer about a possible reduction in your premium given you will be spending a much greater amount of time at home, thus improving security. Cars, on the other hand, may warrant a small increase in premium, though you could also discover that you already have cover within your existing policy.

The other people we should consider telling that we intend to run a business from home are:

- *Local authorities.* Although it is the correct thing to alert your local authority, many would turn a blind eye anyway. The people the rules are designed to capture are those setting up something like a car showroom, day nursery or mini supermarket, all of which will significantly increase traffic and footfall. Using a back room to administer your affairs will hardly be objected to.

- *Mortgage companies and landlords/ladies.* Many mortgage agreements include a clause banning the use of the property for business without consent. Once again, these guys are worried about you changing the use and nature of the property in a way that will affect its valuation and their investment. In most cases, a simple phone call will suffice.

## CHARGING YOUR BUSINESS?

Back to the other considerations of using your home or car. If you use your home for administrative or any other business purposes, is there an argument to charge your business for this privilege?

Crudely speaking, the revenue method of calculating this value is to divide the monthly running costs by the amount of space you are using as a percentage of the whole house divided by the amount of time you use the space.

However, there is another way to calculate this value. Say you were to rent an office in your local area and the total monthly cost was £300. Because you're using your home instead of incurring this £300, is there not an argument to charge the business a similar amount?

The same applies to cars: if you intend to use your car for business purposes then the government sets the amount of money the business can repay you for the use of your car. This is 45p per mile up to 10,000 miles and 25p per mile thereafter. You are expected to cover all the fuel, maintenance, tyres, etc. for the car out of this sum, but providing you are not running around in a Porsche just yet you will find that the deal is fair and in some cases can work in your favour. The records you need to keep are not petrol receipts but mileage logs.

The other option is to buy the car through the business, but now you'll face additional personal tax as this is viewed as a benefit in kind. According to my friends in the accountancy profession, the smart money is on people still retaining ownership of the vehicle, not buying it through the business.

## WORKING HARD, HARDLY WORKING

Understandably, most start-ups will use their home as the initial base for the business. It's cheap, accessible and convenient. Be careful, though: convenience is a double-edged sword. Working from home usually requires far more discipline than a normal working environment.

When we go to a place of work, we cross a threshold that separates work from the rest of our lives. We walk over that threshold at 8 or 9am and reverse the process at 6 or 7pm. So if you're intending to work from home, coming up with a similar division can go some of the way to helping out. But you'll still need to be iron-willed at times.

Starting in business and working from home can be a lonely process, so it's always worth looking at some of the alternatives – either as a different approach entirely or to help divide your time. Many local authorities promote start-up or incubation units that provide a small space, often co-occupied with other people at a similar stage in the trading cycle, heavily discounted or even free in some cases for the first six months. Check out your county or city council website. In my experience, local authorities are very helpful when it comes to start-ups.

If there are no start-up facilities in your area there are some other options to get you out the house: most hotels, for instance, will welcome you sitting in their lounge or coffee areas for long periods. You make the place look busy and perhaps buy the occasional refreshment. I know two professional gamblers who sit all day on their laptops in the main foyer of a leading hotel chain. This is one of the reasons why Costa and Starbucks are so busy during weekdays. Most of the people in there are either retired or conducting some kind of business.

Serviced offices, like those offered by Regus, are another option. These are very nice but not cheap. Some banks, however, offer one-year free membership deals for these sorts of places, so keep your eyes open.

If you visit the cosmetic floor of John Lewis, you'll see lots of stands and brands. None of this stock is owned by John

Lewis but by the brands that occupy the space. This is called a concession arrangement. Can you think of a space that someone has that you could share? Even better if your service complements theirs and vice versa. This happens in hair salons quite a lot, with a nail specialist set up in the corner.

# MONEY MUMBO JUMBO

# THREE

As a former innumerate sales manager selling black socks to Tesco, I was often blinded by the jargon spoken by people in finance. When it comes to the law, it seems to me that a solicitor takes your information, translates it into a language you don't understand then charges for translating it back to you. Finance is often the same; accountants can provide a service cloaked in mystery.

While I am not going to turn you into mini-accountants in this part of the book, I can at least provide you with some foundational knowledge, and strip away some of the mystique, so that you can hold a meaningful conversation with a finance provider or professional.

# 13. GETTING FUNDING

THE FIRST THING YOU NEED TO RECOGNISE IS THAT there is a whole matrix of finance available subject to how much you need, what you want it for and whether you have a good or poor credit score:

- self-financing (personal funds, family, friends)
- bank finance (loans, overdrafts)
- loan guarantee and enterprise funds
- business angels (typically interested in proven businesses)
- factoring, invoice-discounting
- Prince's Trust (under 30) and PRIME (Prince's Initiative for Mature Enterprise).

## FAMILY FINANCE

Naturally, the cleanest form of finance is your own or from a family member. It's inexpensive, it's low-maintenance, it's relatively easy to access and it's less painful emotionally and financially. The other point to stress is that any third-party investor or funding provider will look very favourably on *any* level of contribution made by you.

People think that unless they can match the amount an investor or bank is making they won't get the money. This is not true. Whilst some banks would like a 50/50 split, it is not a deal-breaker.

Believe it or not, banks and other financial institutions will value any time and effort you have already spent on the business and regard that as a personal contribution. Any tangible expenses you have incurred before you started should not be ignored either. Once again, banks will value this contribution. I bought a business in 2002. The business was valued at £1.5m. My contribution was less than 3%. The rest was funded through banks and venture capital (not necessarily a good thing – more later).

## LENDERS

Once you've exhausted the piggy bank, you're now into borrowing – but even here you have a number of options.

The most common and visible form of lender is a bank but it's a mistake to think that one size fits all. Different banks have different opinions of certain sectors. For example, HSBC might be happy to talk about a construction opportunity but Lloyds may not touch it with a barge pole. RBS might be happy to lend you £3,000 for that coffee machine for your café but Santander may only be prepared to lend £1,500 against the same item.

Like many services, you need to shop around. As with insurance, banking can be competitive and with recent changes to account-switching rules, it's hopefully about to get even more competitive.

A common error made by people unfamiliar with banks is to ask for the wrong product. This is evident once again on *Dragons' Den*. The unfortunate quivering wreck has just asked one of the investors for money to pay for items or assets that a bank would typically fund, not a venture capitalist – i.e. a dragon. You need to understand the different types of product offered by banks and what they are designed to pay for. Too many people have let themselves down even before the tea and biscuits arrive by asking for the wrong product to pay for the wrong item.

## LOANS AND OVERDRAFTS

The most common products offered by banks are loans and overdrafts. It's important to recognise the characteristics of each before choosing which one is right for you and your business needs.

*So what is the main difference between a loan and an overdraft?*

Imagine a shop and what you need to set one up: fixtures, fittings, van, till, counter and other 'capital equipment' as it's called. These items would normally be paid for by a loan. A loan is set over a fixed term, say three years, and broken down into fixed and agreed monthly repayments.

Of course, a shop also normally needs stock. So let's say you buy enough stock to furnish your shelves at a cost of £5,000 on opening day. You've successfully negotiated a loan from RBS to buy the stock. The monthly payment is £50. Things start really well and you sell 50% of your stock in the first week. Although your stock holding has reduced to £2,500, you still have a loan of £5,000. Not good. This is where overdrafts are useful.

Overdrafts adjust themselves according to the amount you need at any one point in time. That's why you hear overdrafts referred to as 'facilities' – you have the facility to draw down any amount at any time, up to the limit agreed with the bank.

When I receive income, my overdraft reduces accordingly (i.e. is paid off). For this flexibility, overdrafts can sometimes be a little more expensive than loans. Of course, the other thing to remember is that overdrafts normally fund 'working capital', or the flow of money you need for the business to trade. So, other than stock, there is often no way for the bank to protect itself against its exposure, making overdrafts again more expensive.

BEST-KEPT FINANCE SECRETS

I suspect not many readers will be familiar with loan guarantees or enterprise funds. These are two of the best-kept secrets of finance land. Unfortunately, though banks have access to them, they are also often ignored or discarded as being too painful or difficult to process, leaving you with no option following a refusal.

The enterprise finance guarantee is probably the best-known loan guarantee scheme. It is simply where the government provides security to the bank for your business loan. The biggest single challenge you will face when borrowing money is to provide the lender with some kind of security – in other words, a safety net if something goes wrong, or something they can sell to get their money back. With the enterprise finance guarantee, the government steps in to provide it.

The arrangements for the loan are still down to the bank lending the money. Where the pain comes in for them is the paperwork they have to complete to get the loan secured by the government. To avoid this pain, many lenders have been known to ignore the option and lend the money regardless. Scary!

Enterprise funds are slightly different. Like banks, they have the ability to lend money. Be careful, though: these are not grants. They are inexpensive loans on favourable rates that *still need to be repaid*. The other distinction is that people with poor credit ratings can access these funds.

The most popular example of an enterprise fund is probably the Start Up Loan Scheme (**www.startuploans.co.uk**) created by the British government and headed up by the not-very-young Lord Young. The great thing about the Start Up Loan Scheme is that it comes with compulsory mentoring and business coaching. Given the huge shortage of real-world business support these days, this is a welcome development.

## BUSINESS ANGELS (AND DEVILS)

As mentioned earlier, I bought a business in 2002. I'm not a mergers and acquisitions tycoon – I was part of a management buy-in team that acquired a sports equipment business in Cambridgeshire. Eight months later, I sold my shares back to the former owners at no profit and extracted myself from the business.

The main reason for this was that I had completely misunderstood what it meant to be involved with venture capitalists.

As the name would imply, venture capitalists are gamblers, people who finance or invest in a venture or new product. They're sometimes called business angels – and some can indeed be angelic. Others, less so.

The money is high risk, so it is expensive and normally requires you having to give up large amounts of your business in return. As I found, this is not only expensive economically but emotionally.

One of the main attractions to having your own business is that you control it and direct it. You are deprived of this freedom if you choose to work with venture capital. This means that it should be your last resort, something you only turn to once you have exhausted all other forms of finance.

People go on *Dragons' Den* too eagerly; the dragons are venture capitalists in all but name. Most people appearing on the show do not actually need the help – the cleverest just use it as an excellent promotional vehicle (and there's nothing wrong with that).

## FACTORING IT IN

One form of finance that's both useful and appropriate for start-ups is invoice discounting or factoring. Once again, it is a closely guarded secret in bank land and, subject to the bank, can be restricted to businesses that have reached a certain size measured by sales value.

One of the main challenges when you start is getting credit – i.e. getting someone to sell you goods without having to pay for them on delivery or even before delivery. The other challenge is getting your customers to pay as quickly as possible. Most business-to-business (B2B) transactions work on 30 days credit. In other words, you deliver something today and they pay you in 30 days. One of the tricks in business is to narrow the gap between when you get paid and when you need to pay out. *This is called cash flow management.*

No smoke and mirrors are involved: most of you will already do this in your domestic affairs. The challenge is to stretch your creditors (suppliers) and reign in your debtors (customers). Some businesses have the luxury of getting paid before they need to pay their suppliers. When was the last time you went to a supermarket and instead of paying for your shopping you asked if you could pop back in 30 days and pay for it then? Try it and see what answer you get! Meanwhile the supermarkets in some cases stretch their suppliers to 120 days…yes, 120 days! These businesses are called "cash positive".

Nevertheless, you may not be a supermarket or hairdresser and therefore you may still end up with a gap between suppliers and customers. That's where factoring comes in. Factoring is a device offered by most banks. Whenever you raise an invoice to a client, instead of waiting for that invoice to be paid by your customer, the bank pays you.

Naturally, the bank now adopts the debt and therefore the risk of recovering the debt, so it's no surprise to learn that there is a charge. That's why it's also called invoice discounting. So if you raise an invoice for £100, the bank will typically pay you £92, taking £8 (8%) for the service.

## FREE MONEY

It is clearly in everyone's interest to exhaust any free money or grants that are available. Unlike loans, grants do not need to be repaid. The problem with providing people with information about any free money like this is that there are so many grants out there – and getting hold of them can be such a minefield – that advisors like me tend to run away from mentioning them.

The first thing to recognise is the common ground between each grant. Pretty much every grant uses the same filtration system: Who are you? Where are you? And who benefits?

Each of these questions will lead towards different pots of money – some relevant to you, some not. So use these questions to narrow down your search. Who are you? Have you got a condition of some kind? Are you an ex-service person? Are you 16–24? You can see how it will impact the process. And where are you? Do you live in a disadvantaged area? Do you live in an area already chosen for grant funding? Are you setting up a business in a regeneration zone, a shop for example? And who benefits? As we explored earlier, does your business or enterprise benefit a community or specific groups of people?

Before hunting through Google for grants, ask these questions yourself. It will help you filter through the thousands of grant providers before they start trying to filter through you.

Once you have located a provider that you think may be worth exploring further, it's worth considering the next stage in the process. Grants usually work on eligibility criteria and they are normally split into two categories.

1. Does my personal profile fit the criteria, i.e. age, location, gender, business sector, member of the human race, etc?

2. What the grant is designed to pay for. Regrettably, grants have very strict criteria to prevent you spending the money on a trip to Disney Land. Many grants are very prescriptive about the items or services you can buy with the grant. The final thing to remember is that banks have a vested interest in lending money. The custodians of grant funding often need more persuasion to release the money. The process can therefore be surprisingly more painful than with banks and may take a longer period of time than your business can afford.

# 14. PROFIT AND LOSS

ONE OF THE AREAS THAT MOST STRIKES FEAR INTO the hearts of new businesses is finance and forecasting. Unfortunately, the task is not made any easier by the professionals – i.e. accountants – who, a bit like lawyers, take your information, translate it into their own language and then charge you to translate it back again.

Fortunately, as you are about to find out, it is not as confusing or complicated as you think.

To make further sense of this weird and wonderful world, I'm going to use a range of standard tools typically used when developing financial forecasts for your business. These include the profit and loss statement, sales forecast and cash flow forecast. We'll start with a profit and loss (aka P&L) statement.

The striking thing about the P&L statement is that it is made up of five lines. The confusion develops because, subject to who you are talking to (normally either a bank or an accountant), they are all capable of using different terms to describe each of the lines. So, beginning at the top:

1. Sales, *AKA: turnover, revenue, income, top line*

2. Direct costs, *AKA: COGS, materials, variable costs*

3. Gross profit, *AKA: margin, contribution*

4. Overheads, *AKA: admin expenses, fixed costs, indirect costs*

5. Net profit, *AKA: bottom line, EBIT (earnings before interest and tax).*

**No.1.** Sales. The sales or turnover line represents the amount of money the business plans to generate. We'll look separately at constructing a sales forecast shortly. Even if you are VAT registered, which we'll also look at later, the sales line should not normally include any VAT. It will be before the VAT is added, i.e. net of VAT.

**No.2.** Direct costs. People often get confused between direct and indirect costs. It is a simple but important distinction. Imagine you're a housebuilder. Consider the costs you will incur: bricks and mortar. The more houses you build, the more bricks you will need – this is a direct cost of sale. On the other hand, imagine you are paying someone a flat salary to promote and sell your houses. This person will be paid the same salary whether they sell one house or ten. This is a fixed or indirect cost.

**No.3.** Would it be a good idea from a business management point of view to have a fix on the relationship between the direct cost of sales and sales? As you will see later, any reduction you can make to the cost of sales can have a significant effect on the business. You often hear a dragon (usually Peter Jones) ask "What's your contribution?" and because the quivering wreck has received very little business support, the whole pitch falls apart. Experienced business people can see at a glance whether a business is performing well simply by looking at the ratio between sales and cost of sales. *This measurement is called gross margin.* It is simply sales minus the cost of sales, which gives you a value. A margin is the percentage of this value compared with sales.

**No.4.** Overheads. Many businesses won't even have direct costs because they don't buy bricks to build houses; they may simply be a service business. They will, however, have overheads or fixed costs. These are costs, as described earlier, that start the minute you switch on the lights, whether you sell a house or not. Overheads usually include a whole list of these kinds of expenses, including:

- salaries
- travel/subsistence
- rent/rates
- utilities
- depreciation
- postage/stationery
- professional fees
- bank charges
- IT
- printing and marketing materials

- marketing

- advertising.

One item worth noting on this list is depreciation. Depreciation is a curious calculation. Say you buy an iPad for £500 in your first year of trading. The likelihood is that the iPad will be worth less the following year and may reduce in value. Accountancy rules allow you to anticipate these reductions on certain items; they are normally calculated as reducing in value by a third each year. This then becomes a cost to the business and is entered as an overhead expense. So the iPad depreciation would be ⅓ of £500 until it is written off after three years.

**No.5.** The business end. Net profit. The first place anyone looks when reading your plan. Obviously calculated by subtracting the overheads from the gross contribution. This is why business recovery experts, *Dragons' Den* bods and others attack the easy target of overheads in the first instance to improve business performance. But actually what dramatically affects the performance of any business is the gross margin. When you think about it, overheads by their nature are usually relatively stable. They only really grow relative to the growth of the business. Therefore, if overheads remain stable but gross margin increases significantly then happy days…more net profit.

From a business-management perspective, whilst it's important to always control overheads, your time is much better spent on improving gross margin. There are only a couple of ways I know to improve gross margin – to inflate your prices or reduce your direct costs of sale. Don't underestimate the impact this can have. The table below illustrates this. Whilst overheads remain governed, a tiny gross margin profit improvement has a massive impact on the business performance. I was once told by Peter Doyle of Warwick University that the principal purpose of marketing was to increase prices – when you look at the impact this can have, you would have to say he wasn't wrong.

|  | NOW | 10% PRICE INCREASE |
|---|---|---|
| Sales | £300,000 | £330,000 |
| Costs | £150,000 | £150,000 |
| Gross profit | £150,000 | £180,000 |
| Overheads | £60,000 | £60,000 |
| Profit | £90,000 | £120,000 |

Another closely guarded secret in business is to scale the business without significantly increasing the overheads. Imagine if your turnover doubles at the same gross margin contribution but your overheads remain relatively static. Happy days! All that extra gross profit is converted to net profit. Yippee.

## HOW TO REALLY FORECAST SALES

The most important line on a P&L is of course the top line. Too many people use either a crystal ball or a finger in the air to estimate their sales in the first year. Whilst sales forecasting is more of a black art than a science, there are a number of things you can do to reduce the inaccuracy of sales forecasting.

**Rule number one is to avoid TOP-DOWN forecasting.** I wish I had a pound for all the people who have gone along to a bank and plucked a number out of the air. Once again you will have seen this on *Dragons' Den* – "errrm…about £200,000 I think, no…£300,000" – suicide.

**The second rule is to adopt the principle of BOTTOM-UP sales forecasting.** This is a much more time consuming and painful process but, as someone who used to forecast how many black socks I'd sell to Tesco, I can tell you it's a necessary process.

So, the first thing you need to do is break down your sales to the smallest bite-sized chunks. For example, if you're producing desserts for local restaurants or cafés, each dessert might have a different spec and therefore different price point. Even people who conventionally charge by the hour should try to estimate how many jobs they would need (at that hourly rate) to reach the level of income needed to make the business sustainable

Once you have broken down your list of services, products and the prices that apply to each, the guesswork begins. Naturally, if you have little in the way of forecasting experience or your business has been trading for a short time you will not have any historic records to use. You may need to rely on some common sense, i.e. how many days in the week, how many hours in a typical day, market capacity and your capacity. Once again, the temptation is to start with six months or three months or even one month. Like I said earlier, you need to break down your sales forecast into the smallest bite-sized chunks – so I would like to know what you are going to deliver, sell or make on Monday, Tuesday, Wednesday and so on.

I'd then like to know what you think you can sell in the week after, until eventually you arrive at a monthly figure. You can then cut and paste to arrive at a quarter, six months, 12 months, etc.

Personally, I am not a fan of plans that forecast much beyond two years. Banks and other providers may differ but ask RBS where their business plan is that was written in 2008.

Like I said, this can be a painful but necessary process and unfortunately you have not yet finished. Most people that do a lot of sales forecasting will tell you that putting it down, reviewing it, testing it, showing it to friends and colleagues and having them challenge it, is very much part of the process. They're right.

Now that you have constructed a flat profile, you need to test it robustly. Are there enough days in the week? Is it worth getting out of bed for that many? What about seasonality or other external reasons to expect either a reduction or increase in sales?

If I were running a wedding photography business, for example, I'd expect to see a profile like this:

**JAN FEB MAR APR MAY JUN JUL AUG SEP OCT NOV DEC**

When someone asks you for your break-even, they simply want to know what level of sales you need in order to make no profit or incur no loss. In other words they're looking for a sales figure.

## THE VITAL DIFFERENCE

Believe it or not, I have seen some business plan templates provided by banks described as 'sales and cash flow forecast'. For reasons I'm about to explain, you'll realise that these are two different things.

Naturally, your sales forecast reflects when you think you might deliver or when a client engages with your service. The likelihood is that, shortly after you make the sale, you will create an invoice. But not many places will accept invoices instead of cash, so until you get the money in, the job is only half done. Meanwhile, you have costs, charges and overheads to cover, which are often unsympathetic to whether you have been paid by your customer or not. Here's where the important distinction between sales and cash flow forecasting comes in: cash flow attempts to plot when you think the money is *actually going to come in and when it's actually going to go out.* Banks fixate on cash flow forecast less because they are concerned that you will run out of cash and more so that they can sell you a product to fill the short-term hole. But you need to focus on it so that you don't end up going accidentally bust.

## KEEPING YOUR BALANCE

The only other document you come across occasionally as a start-up, particularly if you choose the limited company route, is a balance sheet. Again, shrouded in smoke, mirrors and wizardry, but it really only serves one purpose. Let's say the business detailed earlier was up for sale – would you buy it? A healthy turnover, low overheads and good net profit ratio.

Not a bad little business, perhaps. But how do you see from looking at the P&L account that this business isn't massively in debt and owes HMRC £50m? You don't. That's why you need a balance sheet.

But don't be misled – all this bit of paper does is tell you what the business owns and what it owes. What it owns is called assets and what it owes is called liabilities.

# 15. THE MAN IN THE BOWLER HAT

IN THIS CHAPTER WE ARE GOING TO RETURN TO THE two most common choices of business types – sole traders and limited companies – and look at the tax implications of each.

Before we separate the two, let's look at the common ground: you can use your personal allowance,[1] you can register for VAT, you can employ people including family members and you can recover pre-start costs.

Now the differences.

---

1    The personal allowance is the amount you are able to earn tax-free. In other words, you will only pay tax when your profit goes over this amount, and only on that profit. This allowance can vary from year to year.

## TAX AND THE SOLE TRADER

Let's look at an example of the tax position for a sole trader. Using a simple P&L described earlier, let's say you make £30,000 sales in the first trading period of your business. Let's also say that you are in catering and your cost of those sales or *variable* costs are running at 20%; therefore your gross contribution or gross profit (GP) will be 80% or £24,000.

Before you move to your overheads, if this is the first year of trading, are there some additional costs you need to work into you calculations? Yes – start-up costs!

Let's say for the purposes of this exercise that start-up costs were £3,000. Then you have other overheads of, say, £10,000, resulting in a pre-tax profit of £11,000. Remember also that, as a sole trader, your overheads do not include any salary for you and that any profit you make after subtracting all the costs is regarded as your salary. This does not prevent you from paying another member of the family or household providing *you can evidence* both the payments *and* that they are doing an appropriate amount of work for the level of reward. The well-publicised cases in the media involving MPs only ever became cases because they could not prove the people they had paid had done any work.

The following table shows a typical first year for a sole trader. For illustrative purposes, the table uses the 2013–14 personal allowance figure and and pre-start costs of £3,000.

| Turnover | £30,000 |
|---|---|
| Cost of goods and services (COGS) | £6,000 |
| Contribution (towards overheads) | £24,000 |
| Start-up | £3,000 |
| Overheads | £10,000 |
| Profit | £11,000 |
| Personal allowance | £9,440 |
| Taxable | £1,560 |
| Income tax @ 20% = | £312 |
| Class 4 NI @ 9%* = | £292.05 |
| Class 2 NI @ £2.60 = | £140.40 |
| Total liability = | £744.45 |
| Net after-tax income = | **£10,255.55** |

* Class 4 NIC is earnings-related and is payable on taxable profits over £7,755 – this is the threshold for 2013–14. It increases annually but is much lower than the tax allowance.

**Remember: profit is gross profit minus your overheads.**

Many people are fearful that becoming self-employed or legitimising a hobby or interest they may have means that they will be paying loads of tax. However, as the table illustrates, this is not the case. What many people miss is that you are allowed to earn a certain amount of money without paying any tax. This is called your personal allowance. At the time of publication, the standard personal allowance in 2014–15 will be £10,000, rising to a proposed £10,500 in the 2015–16 tax year.

The illustration also shows the level and type of National Insurance a self-employed individual pays. i) Class 2 National Insurance (£2.70 per week as at publication) ii) Class 4 National Insurance calculated as a % of profit (9% as at publication). To confuse matters, the Class 4 allowance is much lower than the tax allowance (£7,755 versus £9,440). This needs to be considered in the calculations.

## TAX AND THE LIMITED COMPANY

Using the exact same figures, let's see what the tax might be like as a limited company. The first thing you notice is the overheads have increased by £9,681. This is to allow for a salary of £9,440 (equivalent to the amount you can earn before paying tax) and a small amount of employer contribution.

| | |
|---|---|
| Turnover | £30,000 |
| Cost of goods and services | £6,000 |
| Contribution (towards overheads) | £24,000 |
| Start-up | £3,000 |
| Overheads | £19,681 (inc. Salary and Employer's NIC of £9,681) |
| Profit | £1,319 |
| Corporation tax @ 20% = | £263.80 |
| Employers' NIC = | £240.67 |
| Employee's NIC = | £202.20 |
| Total liabilities = | £706.67 |
| *If the profit left in the company after paying corporation tax is drawn as dividend the net personal income would be:* | |
| Salary £9,440 less employee NIC £202.20 = | £9,237.80 |
| Dividend drawn = £1,319 less corporation tax paid £263.80 = | £1,055.20 |
| Total net after-tax income = | **£10,293.00** |

It is a small difference in this example, but using a company to arrange your income has enabled you to reduce your overall tax costs. Also, the government is introducing an employment allowance to help with the cost of employer's NIC, so in this example the allowance would reduce the NIC cost from £240.67 to £zero.

But before you blaze a trail to Companies House, remember there will be additional costs and admin linked with running a limited company.

## VAT'S UP?

Finally, before you lose the will to live, let's talk briefly about VAT.

First of all, a quick lesson in how VAT works. Try to imagine VAT sitting as a separate layer above both your sales and your costs. Once registered (more on that in a second) you will not have the luxury of choosing which suppliers to pay and which customers to charge VAT. For example:

You generate a sale @ £100 + VAT (20%) = Total invoice value is £120 (£20 VAT)

At the same time you buy an item @£50 + VAT (20%) = Total cost is £60 (£10 VAT)

Then every quarter you add up all the VAT on sales (£20) and all the VAT on costs (£10) before subtracting the costs VAT from the sales VAT. Using this example, that would leave you with £10 credit, which you then send to HMRC. Simple. If you are a VAT-registered business trading with other VAT registered businesses, each is able to offset VAT against the other.

But what if your client is not a VAT-registered business but a private individual? Worse, your nearest and dearest rival is not VAT registered like you? Problem! Because you are now VAT-registered, you have no choice but to charge your customers VAT. You have just inadvertently increased your prices to anyone not VAT registered by 20%. You are therefore likely to lose business in a price-competitive service or market.

Now, you may not have a choice about registering for VAT. HMRC is keen to emphasise that anyone who reaches £81,000 (turnover threshold as at publication) in a rolling 12-month period must register for VAT. Everyone else gets a choice. Is it ever worth it?

That all comes down to how much VAT it would allow you to offset. Some kinds of businesses will need to buy lots of products or supplies that carry VAT – without the ability to offset these costs, they will lose money. So, even though they might have a turnover below the HMRC figure, it can be worth signing up.

However, if you complete returns using the traditional method and VAT on sales is less than the VAT on costs, you will enter a negative return, showing HMRC owed you money. Moreover, going back to the pre-trading expenditure mentioned above, if you have VAT receipts to evidence the VAT in those costs then you may be able to claim it on your first VAT return, and guess what…HMRC will pay it back.

*Note:* There is nothing preventing you from trading then registering for VAT some time later, whether on a voluntary basis or because you reach the mandatory registration limit, but you cannot register for VAT before you have started to trade, as the VAT number needs to be attached to a business.

# 16. MONEY MANAGEMENT

B EFORE WE MOVE ONTO WHAT IS FAR AND AWAY THE
most important aspect of any business in part four, a short
word about financial management, accountancy, bookkeeping
and banking.

## PROFESSIONAL PERIL

While I don't wish to have a go at the accountancy profession,
please don't make the mistake I made in my first year of
business. Drawn by the bright lights and the fancy-dan offices,
off I went with my blank cheque in hand. £2,500 later I realised
I had made a huge mistake. If you feel you need the support of
professional services, try to use an agency or individual – local
and suitably sized. It will save you a lot of money. I'm not
talking about someone 5'11" or 16 stone, I'm talking about a
provider whose business size reflects your own.

Secondly, go with a clear understanding of what you need. Accountancy services are no different from any other business: they will try to sell you all sorts of bells and whistles. As a start-up, all you really need is the preparation of your accounts if you are a limited company or the submission of your self-assessment if you are a sole trader. The only other thing you will need is a payroll system if you have any employees; this can be a bit painful otherwise.

## HITTING THE BOOKS

Try to differentiate between accountancy and bookkeeping: they are two different things. Your 'books' are a record of expenses and costs incurred and a record of sales or invoices. I could find a very strong argument for most people managing this on their own; why would you want to give up the most pleasurable part of your week to someone else – creating invoices!

The more you adopt in this regard, the more you reduce the cost of using outside help. The centrepiece to my early book-keeping system was a bank account. I would encourage everyone to get a bank account even before they're trading, if possible, as this provides an automated record of both money in and money out, which you can then check off against invoices and receipts at various times.

This highlights another important discipline: the big secret behind a good bookkeeping system is *little and often*. A close friend of mine came into the pub complaining that his accountant had quoted him £2,500 for the preparation of his accounts. He was holding a large M&S carrier bag jammed full of receipts. Enough said!

Most high street banks will request you open a business account if they suspect you are running a business. This is not the end of the world as many offer free banking for at least 18 months, and lots of toys.

# HOW TO REALLY SELL

# FOUR

The first three parts of this book are designed to provide you with sufficient knowledge surrounding business formalities for you to start up in business. Unfortunately, too often this sort of thing acts as a distraction from the most important part of any business: actually selling to customers.

That's what we'll cover in this last section. The future of your business will ultimately not be determined by your choice of legal structure but by your ability to generate enquiries and sales.

# 17. THE NON-COAT-BASED APPROACH

W ITHOUT THE ABILITY TO GENERATE CUSTOMERS, enquiries and sales, all the stuff in the rest of this book is largely irrelevant. You can't tax fresh air, at least not yet. We need to generate trade.

In this part of the book we'll explore the real building blocks of many successful businesses. This doesn't come down to whether they are a limited company or sole trader or whether they bank with RBS or HSBC. It's a question of:

1.  Have they got the right proposition or menu of services?

2.  Who are they targeting with this proposition?

3.  Crucially, how do they convey one to the other?

Businesses that get these things right become sustainable, successful businesses. It's important to get away from the idea

EVERYDAY ENTREPRENEURS | KEN HORN

that selling is about opening your coat and asking someone if they want to buy a watch.

Many people are frightened of selling as few have had direct experience of sales and therefore regard themselves as rubbish. **As you'll discover, selling is more about what we do naturally on a day to day basis than pitching at Camden or Leicester market.** It's the ability to hold and work a conversation.

Also, try to split selling from publicity or promotion. These are different things. It is often the combination of these functions that will attract the necessary level of enquiries to make your business sustainable.

Above all, selling is not a fixed thing. Whilst, say, the VAT percentage may vary, the method of calculating VAT doesn't change, nor do many other formalities – so you become more and more familiar with that side of being in business. The thing that does change constantly is the market. You need to be watching it constantly.

Some of the central things that often change are:

- customers' expectations
- ways of selling
- competition.

For instance, in times of recession, there is evidence that people still spend money but want more bang for their buck. This means that we need to build in greater value. *It doesn't necessarily mean we have to increase our costs in the process.* A client of mine buys all her lingerie from one online provider. The provider sells the exact same brands as other online operators, but each time my client receives a delivery, the package includes a single chocolate in a tiny box. This is sufficient to secure her loyalty.

It also follows that the more successful your business becomes, the more competition you will have. As we'll discover later, this is not always a bad thing. But it does need a response.

Another rapidly changing business feature is routes to market. The internet has seen a seismic change in retail and is dominated by some huge operators. However, it may surprise you to learn that even these organisations are worried about what's next and are taking action to defend against potential threats.

# 18. CLIPBOARDS, MOUSTACHES AND MORE

YOU PROBABLY WON'T BE SURPRISED TO READ A start-up advisor saying you need to do research! There are many forms of research you can conduct and we will look at them shortly. Firstly, let's look at the areas we want to find out more about:

- the market
- finance
- customers
- competitors.

The last two areas of research are probably the most important but the others should not be overlooked. Testing and challenging the financial viability of your business is an important issue.

One subject we will look at in this part of the book is price. Everyone is conscious of price having a direct bearing on their business's performance. The wider market, on the other hand, is sometimes ignored. People believe that if they've got customers and competitors marked, the market will look after itself. This is dangerous.

I have seen many businesses get blinkered into only watching their customers and competitors, taking their eye off the broader market, only to find that neither they, the competition or the clients anticipated its collapse. So we always need to have a glancing eye on the market to see what direction it is going in, and whether it's growing or contracting.

Research is typically split into two broad categories: primary and secondary.

Let's get secondary research out of the way, since it's the most straightforward. Secondary research is information or data that you get from third-party sources. There is literally oodles of this stuff out there and you could spend days or weeks trawling through mountains of data and reports.

Such secondary research is all well and good, but for me the stuff that really has an impact is the *primary* stuff: the things you can do. In other words, getting your hands dirty.

There are three or four primary research techniques that I believe most start-ups get huge value from. They can also actually be quite fun.

Here they are:

## 1. QUESTIONNAIRES

The minute I mention questionnaires, I'm sure it conjures up images of standing on a street corner asking random passers-by if they mind answering a few questions.

This is not what I mean.

I'm talking about the prospect of going along to potential *clients* and asking them what they would like from a business like yours. You'd be amazed how many start-ups don't do this and arrogantly and blindly sit in a darkened room second-guessing what a client might want.

Don't do that. Go and ask them.

## 2. CLIPBOARDS AND FALSE MOUSTACHES

This type of research is particularly handy when it comes to finding out about a competitor or speaking to a potential client about the service they currently enjoy from existing suppliers. It's also known as Mystery Shopping.

## 3. SURVEYS

Survey Monkey (**www.surveymonkey.com**) is one of a number of online survey platforms. As someone who has used it myself, I can say that I'm quite impressed but the key to any online survey is the quality of the garbage in versus garbage out.

One problem with surveys is that, under data protection rules, none of the platforms acquires customer data in the process –

and you certainly don't either. The earlier you start to gather this information, with the full consent of customers, the better.

## 4. PILOTING

The final type of primary research is also my favourite. Too often I meet people that have theorised their business idea to death. They have compiled the 90-page business plan but are still crossing *t*'s and dotting *i*'s. Whilst I accept that there is a point when you can jump too early and look daft or under-prepared, there is also a point when you cannot theorise the business any further and need to ask the market. This is called piloting.

Once again, it's always dangerous to assume that you can finalise a comprehensive range of services that satisfy all your customers' requirements without ever seeing if it's true before you fully launch.

The minute you ask customers if you've got it right – by making your stuff available to them – you'll find ways your proposition needs to change. Perhaps only in little ways. But that can be important. It makes you a better business.

# 19. FINDING OUT WHO YOUR CUSTOMERS ARE

T HE CLEARER YOU ARE ABOUT WHO YOU'RE TARGETING, the better you'll be at targeting them. This sounds remarkably straightforward, but you'd be amazed how many people don't do this.

The most successful firms very much do. It's why loyalty cards exist. And it's why supermarket loyalty card departments are staggeringly big. Such customer-monitoring is dressed up as a service designed to help create products and services to better reflect your needs – when in fact it is designed to maximise sales and reduce waste.

Unfortunately you won't have the power and cash of a large supermarket, but you need to understand your clients and potential clients as well as they do. The principles of how to go about doing so are always the same.

## BREAKING IT DOWN

OK, notwithstanding some readers might have an international proposition, for the purposes of the exercise, let's stick with the UK as the marketplace.

According to the latest estimate by the Office of National Statistics, the UK population is just short of 64 million. Given that, unless you're Bill Gates or Simon Cowell, it is unlikely you can target all of these people at once, you need to start breaking this number down.

Start this process by making some broad assumptions about your target groups. Are they male or female? Where do they live? Do they have an age profile? Ethnicity? Wealth?

Already you have fragmented the 64 million into smaller groups and categories. Now ask some more questions designed to distil these groups further such as: profession or job? Kids? Buying habits? Price? Recreational activities? And (my favourite), where do they play?

At the end of the process you should be left with either a clearly defined group or collection of different groups. Don't be alarmed if you have more than one target group. In fact, this is a more sustainable business model; it means you have multiple routes to market. But it also means you are in danger of making another mistake often made by start-ups: that one size fits all.

Let's take the example of a photographer. If you have an eye for taking a good picture you can generally attach this skill to a range of different services and therefore broaden your appeal and routes to market. With this skill you could offer your services to:

- weddings
- events
- portraiture
- press
- advertising.

The important thing is to tailor your approach at all times to the specific customer you're dealing with. Let's say one day you get a phone call from an excited bride and husband to be. They would like a quote for their wedding. You are in a rush that morning and pick up your bumper all-in-one portfolio. After a warm welcome and cup of coffee you flip open your portfolio to pages of…pictures of dead people.

Oh dear.

This is why one-stop shops don't work. This is a pretty extreme example, but the point is that customers and clients never like feeling that you're not specifically serving them. A generalised approach means a net with big holes in that people constantly fall through.

So you need to tweak and tailor your proposition to reflect the specific needs of the specific client. This does not mean that you necessarily need a separate website or trading name for each target – you may just need a separate page on your site for each of them.

Before we move onto competitors, one extra point on customers. Some of you may have heard of the 'Pareto principle' or the 80/20 rule. In short, it suggests that, as your business develops, you will become roughly reliant on 20% of your customers for 80% of your sales.

You can see it in practice in places like Tesco. Once you are in the store, their challenge is to get you to part with more and more of your money by offering you items that either complement what you have already bought or items that, until you saw them, you didn't think you needed. This is also called 'upselling'.

As I mentioned earlier, one of the key challenges you will face when you first start will be securing your first customer. Once you've done that hard work, the next challenge is: what else can you sell them? What else can you offer? But don't forget the other 80% in the process! Some of them may be the 20% tomorrow.

# 20. THE MARKET
# VACUUM

OTHER THAN SPACE TRAVEL, CAN YOU NAME ONE
business Richard Branson has developed that wasn't in
a market already saturated with competition? Music, planes,
trains, hotels, mobile phones and banks – dozens of others had
already got there first.

But it didn't matter.

In fact, it was a very good thing – an important reason that he
succeeded.

This is less paradoxical than you might think. If you go along
to a bank and present two business plans, both asking for the
same amount of money, but one is a hair salon and the other is
for making and selling a brand new widget, which one would
the bank fund?

Easy. The hair salon.

As we explored earlier, banks like safe. Banks like to be able to answer the big question: 'Does it work?' And banks always like it if other people are out there doing something already.

Yes, banks like it if you have competition! What they don't like is a market vacuum.

And you should like competition too. It means you're in a good area – something that's already making money. And it means you have plenty of existing businesses you can learn from. The big question for you is how you become bigger, brighter and better than them. The initial line of attack to achieve this is to understand as much as you can about all aspects of their business, including:

- price
- location
- personnel
- stability
- strategy
- product and services
- weaknesses.

## THE VALUE OF UNDERSTANDING YOUR COMPETITION

A few years back, a client of mine in the Midlands wanted to launch a contract cleaning business. Before he launched, he took my advice and conducted some research on his customers and competition. He chose a large industrial park littered with potential clients and set out on a tour of the park to conduct a questionnaire.

On the questionnaire was a long list of questions designed to build a picture of the people currently providing contract cleaning services. The questions included: How often do they clean? What price do they charge? What time do they clean? Do they use organic products? Are they local? Are they part of a group? (You get the idea.)

Then right at the bottom of the list was the most important question of all and one that everyone, including Richard Branson, needs to ask about the competition: *What are they bad at?*

Anyone who has ever come into contact with the services of a contract cleaning firm knows what many are bad at. The truth is: contract cleaning companies are often bad at cleaning.

The reason contract cleaners don't clean well is because they don't turn up. That's because low pay leads to low morale, which leads to high staff turnover, which leads to poor reliability.

This got my client thinking. *Was he in the contract cleaning business or the turning up business?*

Once he concluded he was really in the turning up business, he started to build his entire proposition around this theme. He put 'reliable' in his business name. Reliability features extensively in his promotional literature and because he is so serious about reliability he even builds it into his terms and conditions. Because he wants to convince every new customer that he is deadly serious about reliability, he offers a cash discount for every time his workforce is either late or doesn't turn up. Guess how many times he has paid it out?

So how come it worked?

There are few businesses more price-competitive than contract cleaning. We'll talk about setting prices later, but he recognised that the customers he was dealing with put value not just on pricing but on punctuality, reliability, responsiveness and guarantees. They were therefore prepared to pay a little bit more. In turn, he passed on most of this increase to staff and therefore pays people higher than any other agency in the area. Now he has a queue of people who want to work for him, staff turnover is low, morale is high, offices are being cleaned well and his business is growing. Simple.

So, as discussed, the two things you really need to know about competition are:

1. Everything.

2. What are they bad at?

# 21. CONSTRUCTING A POWERFUL PROPOSITION

OK, NOW THAT WE HAVE STARTED TO UNDERSTAND who we are targeting and who we are competing with, we're going to look at what we're using as ammunition. What's our offer, proposition or menu of services?

The trick here is to try to broaden your offer without bleeding all over the place. For example, customers regard plumbers as people that bang bits of copper pipe together. The mistake many plumbers make is that they assume customers naturally also associate plumbers with fitting bathrooms, central heating problems, gas appliances, drainage, etc. But most customers don't, so plumbers miss out on all that business.

It's a dangerous mistake.

The other mistake is failing to keep close synergy between the menu items of your business – i.e. you don't really want a business specialising in cake decoration and tree-felling.

## KNOWING WHAT YOU'RE REALLY SELLING

There are a number of layers to constructing a powerful proposition. The first, as we touched on in part one, is to find out what you really sell or the business you are actually in.

This is a vital part of the selling process. Once you understand what you are really selling, it profoundly influences how you sell it and who you sell to.

A few examples:

A bookkeeping client of mine asked herself what she really sold. Lots of new and existing businesses use an outsourced bookkeeping service for two primary reasons. One is security: the comfort that the task has been completed properly. The other addresses one of the challenges most small businesses face in the early stages: time.

Once she concluded she was really selling time, everything else fell into place. Her promotional literature and website had references to time, clocks, deadlines everywhere. Most importantly, once she realised she was selling time, who did she target? People with no time! This made the process of finding clients a lot easier: she targeted single-owner-managed businesses, business consultants, sole traders, etc.

## A MID-LIFE CRISIS BUSINESS

Another great example of a business that truly understands the market it is in and how it affects not only how and who but *how* much they charge is Harley-Davidson.

If you ask the marketing people at Harley what business they are in you'll get a surprising answer.

First, though, who do *you* think Harley competes with? Triumph, Yamaha, Suzuki, Honda, BMW, Ducati? Harley is in the motorbike business, after all, isn't it? If you ask Harley who it competes with they will reply: expensive holidays, divorce, cosmetic surgery, jacuzzis, home improvements.

Harley will tell you they are not in the bike business but in the mid-life crisis business.

Cosmetic surgery is actually another great example of how to think about what you really sell. Many people assume such services are selling glamour, youth, vanity, self-esteem. All those things are involved – but the industry sells something much more fundamental.

The secret is in the method they use to sell it. You've probably seen adverts in the national press, or at train stations, or online. You may detect the use of a particular photographic technique. It's so revolutionary it was once used as a popular children's puzzle. It's called spot the difference. And it shows Before and After.

Instead of portraying the real uncomfortable process of a surgical operation, the cosmetic surgery industry makes a bold display of what it's really selling: change.

# 22. BENEFITS OR FEATURES?

HOW LONG DO YOU HAVE TO CREATE AN IMPRESSION? According to research you have between 7 and 14 seconds before someone will switch off and go elsewhere.

People often think that their CV should merely chart their life story, leaving employers to decipher how it can add value to their business. It's astonishing. But the same happens with businesses and selling their propositions too.

The thing is, customers are not really interested in your business's history – not at first. At first, everywhere and always, *they want to know what's in it for them.*

It's not just the *what* it's the *so what!*

Sales experts will tell you this is the difference between benefits and features. Features are the functionality of a device or the expertise of a consultant but it's *how* the device or expertise is going to affect and bring value to a customer that is all they really care about.

## CONVERTING FEATURES INTO AN ANSWER

I had a client who had worked for a leading aerospace company for 25 years. He had accepted voluntary redundancy and set himself up as a consultant. He put together a fantastic CV chronicling his life history since the age of 12. It was a CV to die for. In particular, he had a lifetime of training in all the productivity-improvement techniques: Sigma, Lean, JIT, etc.

He then spent three months distributing this CV to agencies, small businesses and large corporates. And the phone never rang.

At that point he came to see me. It was time to review his offer and approach. We put together a very short email designed to be read within ten seconds. The email began: "I can improve your productivity by up to 11%".

Guess what happened to the phone.

And all we had done was to convert his features into an answer to: '*What's in it for me?*'

Don't worry. A lifetime of experience is never wasted. That's what keeps customers for the long term. Once you have someone's business on the basis of the benefits you offer them, they're then exposed to all the other stuff you are capable of doing. That's how people who hire you for three months end up using you for six years.

# 23. USP? NOT FOR ME!

WHAT IS A USP AND DO YOU THINK YOU HAVE ONE? USP stands for Unique Selling Point. It's a phrase used too often by so-called entrepreneurs and business experts. They say: if you don't have a USP you should forget your business.

This is rubbish.

Once again, what's unique about Virgin Atlantic or Virgin Money? Too many people lie awake at night or pull their hair out trying to identify what is unique about their business. Don't.

Contrary to the Dragons and Alans of this world, in my experience of helping hundreds and hundreds of people to make it in business: *it is not essential to have a USP*. It is good enough to have some kind of competitive advantage or edge that may not be unique.

That's it.

I have countless clients that have started conventional businesses with nothing more than a simple characteristic that distinguishes them from others in their area. It might be that they're female in a male-dominated sector or that they send each customer a small chocolate in a box with each delivery. Nothing unique, just something different – and better, if at all possible.

# 24. OFFER + VALUE = PRICE

SO, WHAT ABOUT PRICE? HOW MUCH DO WE SELL ALL these great benefits for? What are the key considerations when it comes to setting a price?

The dangerous temptation for most start-ups is to link USP with price. In other words, your unique selling point is that you're simply going to undercut everyone else in the market. This is unsustainable and potentially fatal for a number of reasons.

Firstly, whatever business you're in there will *always* be someone prepared to do it cheaper than you. China has been doing this for years. And it will be much more difficult to increase your prices if you start at a very low price point. Because your customers are used to low prices, they are going to resist any large increases.

Of course, no pricing structure operates in a complete vacuum. First of all we need to consider the range of pricing people are typically prepared to pay for a product or service. There are lots of services we buy where we don't always opt for the cheapest available. What keeps us from always going for the cheapest? Simple: value. We think we're getting value, so we're happy to pay.

So wherever and whenever possible we must look to inject value into our pricing. Value does not mean cost, as the contract cleaner and lingerie supplier earlier on found out. When a leading UK supermarket announced a drop in profits the reaction was notable. Instead of cutting costs, slashing prices and putting everything on promotion, this retailer decided to spend £10m on improved customer experience knowing full well that if they entered a price war they'd lose, and there were more ways than one to add value.

# 25. THE SALES PROCESS

O K, WE KNOW WHO WE'RE TARGETING AND WHAT we're targeting them with. Now we need to examine *ways* to target them.

Most people looking to start a business don't have oodles of cash sticking out of their back pockets to spend on advertising and promotion, let alone the £250k for a 30-second ad during *The X Factor*. We therefore need to get creative to devise other effective ways of promoting our businesses.

Anyone who tells you there is a silver bullet to promoting a new business hasn't a clue what they are talking about. It is the combined and complimentary effect of lots of different types of selling, promotion and publicity that is going to generate the level of enquiries you need to make your business sustainable.

## UNDERSTAND THE SALES PROCESS

Before we look at a long list of things you can do, let's spend a couple of minutes understanding the process of engagement and sale. If I produce a nice piece of literature, a poster, a leaflet, a webpage, a business card or an advert, what is its principle purpose: what is it trying to do or achieve?

Well, quite simple: **create awareness**.

So I launch a big campaign to create awareness, comprising many of the devices we'll discuss later. As a result of this campaign, what am I hoping to get or receive as a result?

**An enquiry**.

So my awareness campaign has worked and I receive an enquiry either by phone, email, text, social media or even carrier pigeon. What do I do then? Naturally, I respond. And when the person who made the original enquiry responds to me we have created an exchange between two members of the human race called: **a conversation**.

Conversations are great. They may not go anywhere. But the spooky thing is that they really do. Even if you hardly intend them to. If we can develop conversation with customers, our chances of conversion go through the roof. **Conversations = conversions**.

I'm sure there are sales professional much better equipped than me to teach you how to sell but, as a member of the human race reasonably familiar with the process of developing conversations, I think you may not actually need much training.

What most people *actually* need help with is the early part of the sales process: generating enquiries. The last few chapters cover these. They are not exhaustive – there will be other things you can do to stimulate interest – but if you do all of the following at least half-well, you *will* generate enquiries.

Remember none of these will lead to a sustainable level of enquiries in *isolation*. You need to do all of them. At the same time, the temptation is often to pepper the whole landscape indiscriminately. The problem with this approach is that you will have no way of measuring what is working and what is not. Stage-managing your promotion plan may be a better idea. Have a think about the sequence and timing of each of the things you're going to do.

# 26. THE VALUE OF BACON SARNIES

I'VE SAID IT BEFORE: SETTING UP IN BUSINESS CAN be a lonely pursuit, so get yourself out there. Networking is hugely valuable in a number of ways.

Despite government cutbacks there are still loads of business networking groups and events you can attend to meet people in a similar position or learn from people who have got more established businesses.

It really works. I made the mistake of ignoring the networking thing for the first two years of my business. Now most of my new work comes through this route. There is tons of material online about networking skills, etc., but for me the ability to hold a conversation with another member of the human race is half the battle. In other words, don't over-think things. There is a broad range of event organisers out there, both large and small.

Start with your immediate environment. Most small towns will have their own local business club. I live in a town called Ashby-de-la-Zouch. Ashby has three local business clubs. Meanwhile, it is hard to find three businesses in Ashby.

Business clubs typically hold bimonthly meetings at a local hotel at around 7am and invite a wide range of members, including retailers, landlords, publicans, tradespeople, accountants, etc., to grab a cup of coffee and a bacon sarnie. These are a very useful introduction to the local business community and will help you build up some early potential referral partners.

Then you have the largest, non-virtual business club. If you haven't already spoken to your Chamber of Commerce, do so. As well as holding their own events, the chamber is also *the* platform to discover other events going on in your area.

In between the biggest and smallest there are a large number of networking groups specific to sector, gender or business maturity – ten minutes Googling within your business niche will bring them up.

# 27. SOCIAL MEDIA AND SEO

I F YOU'VE MISSED THE RAPID RISE OF SOCIAL MEDIA in recent years, don't despair but do catch up quick. As a recent convert myself, I'm only too aware of the power of online activity.

So, first things first, if you haven't already got a Twitter account, then get one. If you haven't already got a LinkedIn account, then get one. And if you haven't already got a Facebook account, then…you know what to do.

All these accounts are dead easy to set up and the first trick is not to be afraid of them. The second is *not* to treat them as megaphones. Social media is not at all about broadcasting – about assuming the world is interested in you and your business and telling them what you think they should know. It's about being available and conversational.

Social media is like the world's biggest coffee shop. No one goes there to be sold to. They go to hang out. You benefit by being present and in the conversation – a part of the community, a part of customers' digital lives – but you will never prosper if you swagger in, assuming everyone's there to listen to you go on about your products.

It's much more about chatting with people so that you're in the forefront of their minds when they do come to buy something in your market, and of staying in touch with those who've used and liked your business in the past.

You may have also noticed something going by the name of Google – an obscure service that few have heard of. Unfortunately, you can exhaust an extraordinary amount of money extraordinarily fast on Google ads, which are used to target people searching for stuff similar to what you offer. The more realistic option is to begin the slow-march to the top using other means. This process is called SEO or search engine optimisation.

SEO is one of the dark arts and sometimes best reserved for people who know what they're doing. But there are basics you can master if you're handling your web stuff yourself. The principles change from time to time (Google is always updating its underlying tech), so the best thing to do is to search around online for some recent and reputable blog posts on the topic. There are also plenty of free training courses online and dotted around the country.

*A note of caution with all web stuff, especially social media and SEO:* consider how many enquiries are likely to come through the internet for your type of business versus the amount of resources you devote to it.

Most people just want a website so they can say they have a website, and little business will be generated by people accidentally landing on that page. Websites are often just a second reference point, i.e. someone has seen your poster or business cards and wants to find out a little bit more. Same with social media. That's fine. *But treat it like that when it comes to time and money.*

# 28. WORD OF MOUTH

THERE IS ONLY ONE FORM OF PROMOTION KNOWN to be more powerful than TV. The great news is that it's largely free. It's called word of mouth.

I also like the term 'personal referral'.

Many people ignore or are complacent about word of mouth, dismissing it as something that they know takes place and will develop over time. This is a dangerous mistake.

Word of mouth or personal referral is a scientifically proven method of promoting a business. Why not harness it and accelerate it?

The first thing to do is to get a pen and paper and write down the people that share your space – anyone with complementary and non-conflicting skills or services. I recently worked with a lady setting up a wedding planning business. I asked her to do the same exercise and she came up with 33 different services that went into the delivery of a wedding, including her own. The question was why didn't she know the other 32 service providers? It would help her business hugely.

The formal translation for 'you scratch my back and I'll scratch yours' is **reciprocal trade**. It's been going on for centuries. HMRC don't like it as often no money changes hands. Tradespeople are masters at reciprocal trade: the plasterer speaks to the painter, the painter speaks to the chippy, the chippy speaks to the sparky, the sparky speaks to the plumber and the world goes round.

Once you have identified your allies, it's time to tell them about your business. This is no more complicated than providing them with either business cards or other promotional literature. In time you may wish to build on this relationship by offering some kind of referral incentive. One former client opened a barber shop in a busy suburb of a major city. Before opening, he toured round the other people in the area who were also in the body or cosmetic business, from beauty salons to gymnasiums. Instead of simply dumping a pile of business cards, he signed each one on the reverse and advised each referral partner that anyone visiting his barber shop holding one of these cards would be given a 25% discount.

# 29. POSTERS, FLYERS AND POS

GATHER POS HAS AN ALTERNATIVE MEANING THESE days, especially online, but here I'm referring to point of sale. That is, any kind of display or item that details your services – be it a poster, a postcard, a desktop display, a card holder, etc.

When it comes to placing these, you want to start with those that link up with the people you've identified as allies or referral partners. How many of these people have a space or outlet acting as a shop window to your market? A plumber might want to target DIY stores. A mobile hairdresser should look at beauty salons. A physiotherapist, gyms. And so on.

Once you have exhausted those kinds of places, the next part of the tour is all the places where lots of people sit around staring at walls, namely: pubs, clubs, taxi ranks, takeaways, doctors, dentists, vets, supermarkets, post offices, gyms, leisure centres, salons, barbers, cafés, restaurants.

Top tip: try to create your promotional literature using a range of different sizes! Not everywhere will be able to accommodate an A4 or A3 poster but there may be space for a postcard-sized display. There are many online providers of cheap if not free business literature which you can design yourself online. Don't make the message too noisy or confusing. You simply want someone to act once they see the advert. The content should be digestible in roughly seven seconds flat. I'm serious.

Many people are attracted to dropping flyers. Partly because they think they work and partly so that they feel as if they have done something tangible to help the business. But the trouble with flyers is that the conversion rate is extremely low – *unless* you get a little bit more scientific.

For instance, I have a client who provides a swimming pool maintenance service to residential clients. Strangely, his flyer hit rate breaks all box office records. Why? Because he only drops flyers through the doors of people who have swimming pools. No prizes for guessing how he knows (let me introduce you to Google Maps), but the point is that the more scientific and targeted you are with flyers the higher the conversion rate.

# 30. PRESS AND MEDIA

I'M SURE YOU DON'T NEED ME TO TELL YOU HOW powerful the press and media can be. Any small mention or feature can have a dramatic effect on your business.

The difficulty I face is convincing people that the media, whether local, regional or national, have a genuine interest in good news stories. But they do.

Many people dismiss the notion that the press will be keen to cover their story and therefore don't bother trying to get coverage. Yet I have many clients who have not only harnessed the media but built their publicity and proposition around them.

There are a couple of lessons to be learned from those people who have successfully used the media to promote their businesses.

Lesson 1: Try to give the story a dimension beyond whatever it is you are doing. Try to give the story an angle. This might be connected to your personal circumstances. It might play into an agenda that is particularly hot at the time. Is the story news-worthy and media-sexy?

Lesson 2: The press are incredibly lazy so don't expect them to turn up with their lights, cameras and reporters ready to create the feature. Instead you need to become your own PR department. Images and narrative, packaged together in a tidy piece ready to be cut and pasted with minimal interference. And you need to bang it out to every press and media player from local newspaper to regional and national TV news. This is no time for modesty. You need to distribute as widely as possible. You cannot predict who and when someone will be keen on the story.

Finally, don't give up! Many of my clients who are now well-known to TV and radio report that you cannot anticipate when your story may become relevant to a broader piece being prepared. You need to adopt a shotgun approach. (By which I mean, spray and pray – don't threaten journalists with firearms.)

# 31. LAUNCH EVENTS

HOLDING A SPECIFIC EVENT OR STUNT TO SIGNAL the launch of your business is another effective ploy overlooked by many start-ups. Too many simply get up Monday morning and stumble into trade. Don't.

You can use a launch event to create noise and publicity. Drag in local press and perhaps some of your allied services to join the show. The barber mentioned earlier had been trading for three weeks when I first met him. Trade was very low. So we shut him down and organised a launch day for his return.

We needed something to hook local interest so we decided to offer free haircuts for a day. Needless to say, the place was packed. There was a queue all day outside his shop. Terrific publicity. He also instantly created repeat business.

The icing on the cake came when I received a text from him at 4.30 on the day of the launch. A regional TV company had turned up to film a live piece for the evening news. His shop is busy to this day.

# 32. ADVERTISING

I T WOULD BE WRONG TO TALK ABOUT THE PROMOTIONAL mix without mentioning advertising. Advertising is the most immediate, visible and recognisable form of promoting a business. It is also the laziest option and is consequently expensive.

You can exhaust a lot of money very quickly on advertising, so I'd encourage you to concentrate on the other methods we've explored first. But there are still some cost-effective methods of local advertising. Local radio can be pretty cheap, as can the little electronic displays in shops and post offices, which are often operated by independent companies at a reasonable cost.

One of the most powerful local advertising platforms is the little glossy mag, normally A5 in size, that drops through your letterbox. The striking thing about these is the distribution vs. readership ratio is extremely good. In other words, a high number of people who get one read it. Despite the fact that they are pretty much full of local adverts, they have almost become the antidote to intergalactic Google.

Whatever forms of advertising you eventually go for, be sure to tread carefully. Try not to commit yourself to any long agreements but look to run short pilots to test the impact on your business.

# CONCLUSION:
## REPEATREPEATREPEAT

ONE OF THE BIG CHALLENGES WHEN IN BUSINESS on your own is that you need to continue to promote and sell the business to secure the next order *at the same time* as already delivering your service. I am still doing this today, after starting my business back in 2005.

The good news, as with much business stuff, is that it gets more familiar. It's just a question of repeating the process we've gone through. And repeating it again. And again.

Meanwhile it's always getting a little easier.

Setting up a business *will* stretch most of your abilities, expertise and stamina. But for that reason, it's one of the most rewarding things you'll ever do.

The very best of luck.

**KEN**

# THANKS FOR READING!

We hope you loved this book as much as
the team here at Harriman House.

We'd love to hear your thoughts, so do leave a
review online or get in touch via:

- Twitter – *@harrimanhouse*

- or email – *contact@harriman-house.com*

If you liked *Everyday Entrepreneurs*, we think you'll
also love *The 5-Minute Marketer* by Stefan Ekberg:

**www.harriman-house.com/5minutemarketer**

Lightning Source UK Ltd.
Milton Keynes UK
UKOW07f1215101114

R1394600001B/R13946PG241263UKX1B/1/P

9 780857 193452